How to be a Para *Pro*

A Comprehensive Training Manual
for Paraprofessionals

Other Quality Products Available From Starfish Specialty Press:

Asperger's Syndrome: Crossing the Bridge – VHS Video
Featuring: Tony Attwood & Liane Holliday Willey

Autism Spectrum Quarterly Magazine
Diane Twachtman-Cullen, Ph.D., Editor-in-Chief
Liane Holliday Willey, Ed.D., Senior Editor
www.asquarterly.com

Family to Family: A Guide to Living Life When a Child is Diagnosed With an Autism Spectrum Disorder – DVD
By Alyson Beytien

How Well Does Your IEP Measure Up? Quality Indicators for Effective Service Delivery
By Diane Twachtman-Cullen & Jennifer Twachtman-Reilly

Souls: Beneath & Beyond Autism
By Thomas Balsamo & Sharon Rosenbloom
Book, DVD and Calendar available

Super Silly Sayings that are Over Your Head: A Children's Illustrated Book of Idioms
By Catherine S. Snodgrass

Trevor Trevor
By Diane Twachtman-Cullen

Visit our web site to learn more about the fantastic products:
www.starfishpress.com

How to be a Para *Pro*

A Comprehensive Training Manual
for Paraprofessionals

Diane Twachtman-Cullen, Ph.D.

Illustrations by David A. DeLorenzo

STARFISH SPECIALTY PRESS

Because it makes a difference to this one

P.O. Box 799
Higganum, CT 06441-0799
www.starfishpress.com

Published in the United States of America by Starfish Specialty Press, LLC,
PO Box 799, Higganum, CT, 06441-0799

Book design: Deborah Prater, Image Access; Moodus, CT

Questions regarding this book, including ordering information should be addressed to:
Starfish Specialty Press, LLC
P.O. Box 799
Higganum, CT 06441-0799
Phone: 1-877-STARFISH (1-877-782-7347)
E-mail: info@starfishpress.com
Visit us on the Internet at www.starfishpress.com

Discounts are available for bulk purchases.

ISBN-10: 0-9666529-1-6
ISBN-13: 978-0-9666529-1-8
Library of Congress Catalog Card Number: 00-190003

Printed in the United States of America

First Printing: February 2000

10 9 8 7 6

To Joyce Suffish

who as a Para *Pro* made the world *different* and *better*
because of her inestimable importance in the life of a child

Joyce Suffish: The "Gold Standard" of Paraprofessional Support

A Hundred Years From Now

...it will not matter what my bank account was, the sort of house I lived in, or the kind of car I drove...but the world may be different because I was important in the life of a CHILD.

Author Unknown

A plaque bearing those simple but profoundly meaningful words graces the wall of my home office. They are a fitting tribute to the person who served as my prototype for the Para *Pro* in *How To Be A Para Pro: A Comprehensive Training Manual For Paraprofessionals.* Meet Joyce Suffish, and know that the world is indeed *different*, and *better*, because she was profoundly important in the life of a child named Brandon.

Joyce didn't start out as Brandon's one-to-one para. In fact, she wasn't a one-to-one para at all. A teacher, by profession, Joyce had re-entered the field of education after an absence of several years, during which she had devoted her time to raising her family. Accepting a position as a paraprofessional, Joyce was assigned to Brandon's kindergarten classroom. It was to have been an *interim* position, until such time as she could bring her teacher certification up to current requirements.

Brandon didn't have a para assigned to him. Hence, he was, quite literally, on his own — a situation that left him ill-equipped to deal with the distractions and complexities of an inclusive classroom environment. On the day of my observation, the classroom seemed to swirl about him as he wandered from one enclave of children to another — his presence unfelt and unacknowledged. At one point he sat down in the play area and picked up a toy truck — a solitary figure *among*, rather than *with* children. There was no one there to intervene when a boy, desirous of the truck in Brandon's hands, simply reached over and took it. Had the child learned that sweet-tempered and passive little Brandon would simply acquiesce to the brazen gesture?

Absent the truck, Brandon lost interest in the play corner. He got up and wandered over to the area where the books were housed, a place where he clearly seemed comfortable. I heard an adult's voice say, *"He's very smart, you know. He's learning to read."* It was Joyce. Her face lit up as she talked about Brandon, and her words painted a picture of a capable little boy who was eminently able to learn, if only someone would give him the extra time and help he needed to do so. Clearly, Joyce was that someone, for she saw the child and his substantial strengths, *not* the autism and its weaknesses. Brandon responded to Joyce by giving her the precious gift of his attention.

I left the classroom that day with one recommendation firmly in mind. I called Brandon's parents that night and said, *"Whatever you do, and however you make it happen, you must get Joyce Suffish as Brandon's one-to-one para."* In the years to follow, as the family's consultant, I would make many more recommendations, though none quite so significant as that first one that brought Brandon and Joyce together.

Their first full year together began when Brandon entered first grade. His parents asked me to observe him in his inclusive classroom setting. Despite Joyce's considerable efforts, the pace of the classroom was simply overwhelming. Being in the trenches, Joyce was able to tell me that Brandon's *best* learning took place in the special education resource room, where she was able to slow down the pace of activities, and devote time to repetition and practice. I called Brandon's parents that night with my unwelcome recommendation — Brandon needed to spend far more time in the resource room. Despite their desire for an inclusive classroom setting for their son, their faith in Joyce's instincts, and their interest in their son's well-being prevailed, and for the next few years Brandon received most of his education in the special education classroom.

What a joy it was to see Brandon and Joyce work together. And what a privilege it was to see Brandon grow from a sweet, but somewhat tentative child, into one who exudes the quiet confidence of a learner. Joyce spent 5 full years with Brandon in her "interim" position as a paraprofessional support person. What is most remarkable is that, last year, at the beginning of Brandon's fourth grade experience, Joyce was offered a plum of a teaching position in the same school where she was working — a dream come true by most people's standards — but not by Joyce's! She declined the position so that she could spend one more year with Brandon as his para pro, convinced that fourth grade was — in her own words — "a crucial swing year into the upper grades." When she told me of her decision, I said, "You must know that you have been Brandon's *Annie Sullivan* [the remarkable teacher of Helen Keller]." Her eyes filled with tears at the comparison.

This story has an even more remarkable ending (beginning?!). Brandon is in the fifth grade this year, and Joyce did accept a teaching position, after all. Though *fully included*, and doing *grade-level* work, Brandon doesn't have a one-to-one para — not because Joyce is unavailable, but because for 5 exquisite years she built and fortified the foundation for Brandon's learning, "brick by brick", thus *enabling* him to learn independently.

I spoke to Joyce recently, and asked her what she thought made the biggest difference in Brandon's education. She said, *"I always tried to teach him something every day. Start small and keep building. Make every day count."* How To Be A Para Pro is dedicated to Joyce Suffish, the remarkable woman who became a paraprofessional by circumstance — and *realizing the profound importance of the job* — became a para *pro* by choice! Brandon's father captured the essence of Joyce, most eloquently, in a note he sent to her just a few weeks ago:

> "Whatever others have done, and notwithstanding Brandon's substantial contributions to his own success, you have been the single most significant factor in this miracle. I know that I will never in the course of my professional career do anything as significant as what you have accomplished with him."

May the example set by Joyce be an inspiration to all who have the honor and privilege to *enable* learning for children with autism spectrum disorders. And may the world be *differerent* and *better* because of your importance in the life of the children you serve.

Table of Contents

Acknowledgments

The writing of this manual has been a *labor of love* in every sense of the term—at times tedious, difficult, and all-consuming, while at others, deeply satisfying in the way a warm blanket settles one in on a chilly evening. In recognizing those whose efforts are woven into the fabric of this manuscript, I am reminded of the quotation by Richard Challoner, the 18th century bishop who said, *"Sanctity does not so much depend upon doing extraordinary actions, as upon doing our ordinary actions extraordinarily well."* It occurs to me that *excellence* works according to the same principle. Thus, I am grateful to the many people who lent their excellence to this endeavor by performing their "ordinary actions extraordinarily well."

My thanks to Joyce Suffish for her example, and to other para *pros* whose excellence helped to inspire this manual.

Many thanks to David A. DeLorenzo for his whimsical and endearing illustrations, as well as his patience throughout this project. Thanks also to his parents, Susan and Carl, for taking the time to come to Connecticut so that David and I could work together.

My thanks to the Technical Department of the Hartford Public Library for their assistance.

To Deborah Prater of Image Access, were it not for you, you wouldn't be reading this! Thanks for your creativity, your speed of response, and your enduring patience.

Many thanks also to Beverly Kolouch who helped us to meet our deadlines by taking on much of the burden regarding the tedious preparation of many of the forms and tables.

To Susan Williams, thank you for your illuminating perspectives on paraprofessional support, your editing, and for translating my inexplicable renderings into easy-to-read and adorable stick figures.

I am deeply indebted to Jim Ball, Carol Gray, and Barry Prizant for taking time from their busy schedules to lend their eloquence and support to this endeavor. I am most grateful to you Carol, and the entire staff of *The Morning News* for believing in the importance of paraprofessional support enough to devote an entire issue of your publication to it.

Thanks to my husband Jim for "putting life on hold" for awhile, in deference to this project, and for the opinions and ideas that lent so much to it.

To my daughter, Jennifer, thank you for giving me the precious gift of your time and talent in the editing (and seemingly endless re-editing) of both the wording and content of this manual. Only you could have done justice to both. In many ways, you were my *lightning rod* for excellence!

For my son, Erich, you have been involved in so many phases of this project, that it is difficult to know where to begin to express my appreciation. Suffice it to say that your decisions have helped to shape this project from inception to completion. Without your substantial contributions and superb decision-making, *How To Be A Para Pro* might not have *been* at all!

My heartfelt thanks to all of you for your significant contributions to this *labor of love*.

Foreword

Supports and related services have become an increasingly important part of the educational landscape for students with special needs, both in inclusive classroom and special education settings. More and more often these include one-on-one instructional support staff assigned to specific students. In fact, the numbers of instructional support staff, and the corresponding expansion of their duties and responsibilities, have increased so dramatically that schools throughout the United States have had difficulty meeting the in-service education needs of these critically important members of the school community. This is no small problem, when one considers that the emphasis on inclusion has helped to create an increasingly complex special needs population—one that *requires* comprehensive, ongoing in-service education for its caregivers.

The Federal government has not only recognized the need for support staff training, it has placed *increasing emphasis* on it in the last few years. To wit, the *IDEA Amendments of 1997* acknowledge the importance of appropriate training for support staff who render educational care to students with disabilities. The *IDEA Final Regulations*, published in March, 1999 place even greater emphasis on appropriately trained personnel—both professional and paraprofessional—by holding states to a higher standard whereby they must *ensure* that those who provide services for students with disabilities have an adequate knowledge base and the skills to do so.

In my work as a consultant for children and youths with various types of developmental disorders, particularly pervasive developmental disorder (PDD), autism, and Asperger syndrome (AS), I have had numerous opportunities to observe the important work instructional support personnel do for the students they serve. From this experience I have gleaned the following:

• The success of the student's educational program is directly related to the quality of the service provided by the instructional support person.

• The quality of the service performed by the support person is directly related to the quality of the information and training that s/he has received.

• Given their perceived need to be with their charges, *support staff are often left out of the information/training loop!*

This manual seeks to ameliorate this informational Catch-22 by addressing the critical need for information and basic training which instructional support staff requires in order to work more successfully with their students. While the manual will address noninstructional duties as part of the paraprofessional's responsibilities, it will not address the needs of noninstructional support staff, per se. The primary focus will be on paraprofessionals who provide *direct instruction* to students with special needs, whether in a one-on-one or small group format. In the latter case, a support person may be assigned to two or three students with special needs.

While several aspects of this manual are generic, and hence appropriate to the needs of paraprofessionals working with students manifesting a variety of handicapping conditions, *How To Be A Para Pro* specifically highlights the disability of autism and related disorders, providing comprehensive information that goes well beyond the hallmark features associated with these conditions. The inclusion of this information serves two important purposes: 1) to provide sorely needed information regarding an enigmatic and highly variable syndrome, about which there is much confusion and misinformation; and 2) to serve as a prototype for the type of information support staff needs for students with disabilities other than autism who also present with some degree of cognitive impairment (e.g., Down syndrome, ADD/ADHD, specific learning disabilities, Williams syndrome, mental retardation, and others).

While this manual is specifically designed to address the needs of paraprofessionals—and can stand on its own as a *comprehensive training program*—there are two important ways in which the professional staff can use the manual, as well. The first is as a source of *information*, a use that is particularly germane to the needs of *regular educators* who have children with autism and related conditions in their classes. Special educators and clinical support staff will also find the manual useful not only as a means of increasing their knowledge base, but also for the examples and specific programming recommendations which it contains. The second way professional staff can use the manual is as a means of *supervision*; that is, as a tool by which teachers can *train, oversee,* and generally *guide* paraprofessional support staff in the performance of their duties.

How To Be A Para Pro contains many *reproducible* forms not only to assist support staff in the rendering of more systematic instruction, but also to provide them with the means by which to judge and record student progress. The numerous examples interspersed throughout the manual are intended to "flesh out" programming recommendations so that the transition from printed page to real world application may be made more easily. Toward this end, the manual also contains two important instruments to further promote applicability. The first is a tool for gauging the amount of caregiver support needed to facilitate student performance. The intent of this instrument is to enable caregivers to monitor student support needs so that they may make the adjustments necessary to reduce prompt dependency and promote independence. The second instrument consists of a five-step plan for addressing problem areas with respect to student functioning. Presented in vignette form, this plan provides a "how to" template for remedial support across a wide variety of areas.

Preface

"A Rose By Any Other Name..."

You are known by many different labels. In some school districts you are called one-to-one aides, or simply aides. In others you are called tutors, teaching assistants (TA's), paraeducators, or paras (short for paraprofessionals). You are even known generically as one-to-ones. In a few school districts I've heard you referred to as "follow alongs," and in others as "shadows." Regardless of what you are called, you are those unsung heroes in the trenches. In my own workshops I refer to you affectionately as "trench people" to underscore your crucial "front and center" role in the lives of the students you serve. In the interests of uniformity, you will be known as *paras* in this manual. This prefix from the term *paraprofessional* is an apt one—intended to acknowledge your dual responsibilities to both the students you serve and the teachers you assist. May the information contained within these pages—though rendered in "tongue-in-cheek" fashion at times—enable you to become a real (para) *pro* at what you do!

The Crucial Need for Training: What You Don't Know...

Imagine yourself in the difficult-to-imagine situation of having sustained a serious spinal cord injury in an automobile accident. How well-served would you be by paramedics who have no understanding of, nor training in the care of traumatic injuries? How much confidence would you have knowing that an untrained person's untoward move could mean the difference between full recovery and total paralysis? Or, on a less dramatic note, would you want to have a broken bone set by a dentist, or a root canal performed by an orthopedist?

We live in a society where we expect (demand?) basic competence from people as varied as grocery store clerks and television repair persons. Shouldn't the standard of *basic competence* serve, at the very least, as a *minimal* standard for children and youths with special needs? The basic premise of this manual can be summed up in the following version of the old adage: *What you don't know (about a disability) may not bother you, but it can (and often does) "bother" (i.e., jeopardize) student learning!* For example, lack of knowledge may cause you to expect too much or too little from a student, or to make judgments which *compromise*, rather than *facilitate* learning.

There are few disabilities which require as intense a degree of *informed support* than those which come under the category of pervasive developmental disorder (i.e., autism, Asperger syndrome, PDD, and PDD-NOS). For those who recognize the complexities involved in these conditions, it should come as no surprise to learn that the symbol of the Autism Society of America is that of a child with autism as the central figure in a puzzle—testimony to the enigmatic nature of this multifaceted disorder, and the consequent need for understanding and training on the part of caregivers. Notwithstanding, it is the *paucity* of training opportunities for paraprofessional support staff, in general, that is the standard in school districts throughout the United States—a standard that holds even as the numbers of paras and students with autism and other cognitive impairments increase.

How To Be A Para Pro: A Comprehensive Training Manual for Paraprofessionals is intended as a first step toward rectifying this unfortunate situation, by providing paraprofessional support staff with some urgently needed basic information about autism and the students they serve who manifest it. In a more generic sense, this manual also covers both the crucial role which one-on-one, instructional support staff play in the lives of their charges, and the important duties and responsibilities they must fulfill in order to meet the letter and *spirit* of their "job description." Comprehensive in focus, this manual is both a *basic training course* and a *resource* for specific suggestions for preparing and implementing a wide variety of educational supports.

How To Be A Para Pro is not intended to supplant on-site paraprofessional support training efforts, but rather to *supplement* them where they do exist, and to *inspire* them where they are lacking. Moreover, this manual specifically acknowledges that in-service education should be *comprehensive* and *continuous* in order to be maximally effective. If all else fails, however, and training efforts fall short, this manual can serve as a useful road map to guide you along the paths that lead to effective educational programming for students with special needs.

Take Home Message

- The first most basic building block of appropriate educational programming is *knowledge of both the disability and the student who manifests it*.

- *Ignorance is not bliss!*

- In-service education for paraprofessionals should be *comprehensive* and *continuous*.

R-e-s-p-e-c-t: The Thread of Commonality

There are many different intervention techniques used for children with autism and related disorders. *How To Be A Para Pro* is not intended to endorse nor detract from any one of them. Neither is it intended to provide training in specific methodologies, whether with respect to autism or any other disability. Thus, this manual can be used successfully by *all* paras *irrespective of program philosophy or setting, and regardless of the particular handicapping condition manifested by their students*. It is important to note, however, that this manual does reflect my personal philosophy regarding the education of children with pervasive developmental disorders and, indeed, *all* children. This philosophy can be summed up in one word: *respect*— respect for the child's unique perspective, learning style, and needs. It may be helpful to imagine the enigmatic child with a pervasive developmental disorder as though equipped with the following warning label:

Fragile—Handle With Care

Even though there are many things about me that are unique, in the ways that really matter I am just like other children. I learn best from people I trust, and I learn to trust when I sense that people like me. Please try to see the world through my eyes, for I can't see it through yours. And please know that even though it may not seem so, I really am trying to adapt to a world that my neurological challenges prevent me from understanding without your help. If you keep these things clearly in mind, you will be less apt to label me a *behavior problem*, and more likely to *teach me* the things I need to know so that I can function with greater understanding and competence in a world that is often inhospitable to my needs.

This manual is also written with intense respect for paraprofessional support staff, as well, in recognition of the important role which paras play in the lives of students with disabilities. What you do, and the manner in which you do it matters very much, for as trench people you have the power to *facilitate* learning or to *impede* it. It is important to bear in mind, however, that with power goes responsibility—first to *learn* about the child and his/her needs, and then to *apply* that information in a manner that *enables* learning.

Take Home Message

- From a "big picture" perspective, *what is best for neurotypical children is not only best for children with autism, but also for all children with special needs.*

- *Individuals with autism are operating with their best efforts at adaptation* under difficult conditions, given their neurological challenges.

- In order to effectively meet the needs of students with autism, it is necessary to *view the world from their individual perspectives.*

- *With power goes responsibility*—first to *learn*, then to *apply* information in a manner that *facilitates*, rather than impedes learning.

Format

This manual is designed to be "user friendly" in every sense of the term—easy to read, easy to follow, and easy to reference. To meet this goal, I have tried to present only *fundamental* information in a straight forward, easy to understand manner, uncluttered by all but the most essential explanations and references. To this end, I have studiously avoided footnotes as *user unfriendly*. My main objective was to present you with a manual that is approachable and readable, rather than tedious and cumbersome. *How To Be A Para Pro* is organized in a manner that moves from general information about autism and related conditions, to specific information regarding the use of educational supports to facilitate student learning. The numerous examples interspersed throughout the manual are intended to enhance understanding. User-friendly special features include the specifically intended *overly liberal use of italics* (I couldn't resist!) to emphasize important information. Please consider their extensive use in this manual as the print version of a yellow highlighter pen! *Topic markers* in the margins serve as "heads up" mind joggers regarding content, while *Bottom Line* statements encapsulate important information and help to tie things together. *Take Home Messages* interspersed throughout the manual further highlight and summarize important information.

Part One of the manual is devoted to a "short course" on autism and related conditions. Chapter 1 covers the autism spectrum disorders continuum, and issues related to diagnostic labels. Chapters 2 and 3 discuss the two hallmark features of autism, problems in *social behavior* and *communication/language impairment*, respectively. Chapter 4 covers the way in which autism and related disorders affect the students' interests, activities, and imagination, while Chapter 5 presents information on students' abnormal response to sensation. Chapter 6 addresses theory of mind, information processing, and organizational skills, while Chapter 7 compares high functioning autism and Asperger syndrome.

Part Two of the manual is devoted to the "art and science" of being a para *pro*. Chapter 8 presents a general overview of paraprofessional support for students with special needs. Chapter 9 discusses the duties and job responsibilities of paraprofessional support staff, while Chapter 10 addresses the manner in which these duties and job responsibilities are carried out. This chapter not only takes a tongue-in-cheek look at problem paras and presents the Para Pro, it also details a generic, readily translatable formula for promoting successful student-caregiver interaction. Chapter 11 presents sample accommodations and supports within the framework of direct-application, "how to" vignettes pertaining to students with autism and related conditions. Finally, Chapter 12 presents a "wrap up potpourri" which includes an important "mission statement."

How To Be A Para Pro contains tables and charts to streamline the presentation of information, and includes two Appendices—one that consists of a compendium of Take Home Messages, and another that contains information on valuable resources. A variety of reproducible record keeping forms is also interspersed throughout the manual to make your life easier, and your students' educational experiences more effective.

Take Home Message

Read and *heed* the take home messages!

PART ONE

Autism Spectrum Disorders "101"

A Short Course for
People in the Trenches

Chapter One

Getting to Know Your Student
The Autism Spectrum
Disorders Continuum

There are many different labels that are used to characterize the type of learning difficulty associated with the word *autism*. To make matters more confusing, there is little uniformity in the way these labels are used. For example, some individuals use the term *autism* interchangeably with that of *pervasive developmental disorder*. To others, the two terms represent two separate and distinct disorders. Notwithstanding, there are some things that most professionals do agree upon—that *autism exists on a continuum from mild to moderate to severe,* and that it is a *spectrum disorder;* that is, part of an array of varied but similar entities. Hence, the term *autism spectrum disorder (ASD)* will be used in this manual to encompass the entire continuum. The following schematic incorporates these two ideas:

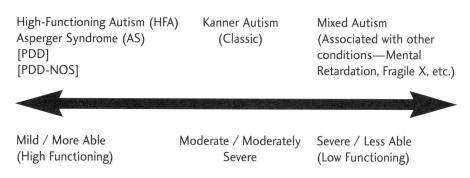

High-Functioning Autism (HFA)   Kanner Autism   Mixed Autism
Asperger Syndrome (AS)   (Classic)   (Associated with other
[PDD]   conditions—Mental
[PDD-NOS]   Retardation, Fragile X, etc.)

Mild / More Able   Moderate / Moderately   Severe / Less Able
(High Functioning)   Severe   (Low Functioning)

THE AUTISM SPECTRUM DISORDERS CONTINUUM

What's in a Name?

As you can see autism, Asperger syndrome, and the PDD's (i.e., pervasive developmental disorder and pervasive developmental disorder not otherwise specified) represent related conditions on the autism spectrum disorders continuum. Generally speaking, when the labels *PDD* and *PDD-NOS* are used they refer to individuals judged to be at the more capable end of the continuum. The *N-O-S* designation is meant to signify that the individual so diagnosed is *atypically* atypical, if you will. In reality, it functions as a "catch all" term, much like the proverbial wastebasket. While the *PDD/PDD-NOS* labels are considered important by some professionals from a research standpoint, for those of us in the trenches, they do little more than confound and confuse. I have included them in the schematic above, however, since they are labels that you will encounter and hence need to put in their proper place, so to speak. I have bracketed them as a gentle protest against their use as *individual* diagnostic categories, for in my opinion, the term *Pervasive Developmental Disorder* would more aptly serve as the overall umbrella designation for the autism spectrum disorders continuum.

The two other diagnostic categories found at the more able end of the continuum are *high-functioning autism (HFA)* and *Asperger syndrome (AS)*. There is even greater confusion surrounding the use of these labels. Some professionals feel that HFA and AS are two separate and distinct conditions. Others feel that Asperger syndrome is nothing more than high-functioning autism. Still others adopt a middle-of-the-road stance, incorporating aspects of both positions into their views. *DSM-IV*, the official compilation of diagnostic categories in the United States, does little to resolve the issue (and, if the truth be known, an awful lot to perpetuate the confusion!). On the one hand, *DSM-IV* lists the *identical* set of criteria for both autism and Asperger syndrome, and on the other, it states that to qualify for a diagnosis of Asperger syndrome, one cannot qualify for a diagnosis under any other pervasive developmental disorder. This suggests a separateness that the symptomatology simply does not support. If you are hopelessly confused, take heart, you're following along beautifully!

Candidly, the cards aren't all in on the relationship between autism and Asperger syndrome, but that won't impede your

Traversing the autism spectrum disorders continuum

work in the trenches if you adopt the following stance: *Autism and Asperger syndrome share many similarities, but there are important differences, as well.* In fact, it is the differences which make programming for children with Asperger syndrome a little tricky. For this reason, HFA and AS will be addressed in greater detail in a later chapter.

Kanner autism—located smack-dab in the middle of the continuum—is so named for Leo Kanner, the physician who first described the syndrome in 1943. It is also the more classic presentation of this multifaceted disorder, and the one that most people have little difficulty recognizing as autism, per se. Descriptions of these children characterize them as being in a world of their own. Terms such as *aloof* and *detached* are often used to underscore their social isolation. Ironically, even though these children are eminently recognizable as having autism, they constitute a relatively small percentage of cases on the autism spectrum disorders continuum. In fact, it is generally accepted that individuals with Asperger syndrome comprise the largest single group of those with ASD, a characterization which school districts across the country can attest to, given the increased numbers of children they are seeing who carry this diagnosis.

At the less able end of the continuum, one finds autism mixed with other conditions such as Fragile X syndrome, Tuberous Sclerosis, or mental retardation. The presence of additional conditions further complicates both the diagnostic picture and educational programming. Further, while it is possible for people with ASD to have an accompanying seizure disorder at any level of cognitive functioning, seizures are more commonly seen in those individuals at the less able end of the continuum.

Finally, it is important to note that *autism can exist with or without mental retardation.* While it is easier, at least on a relative basis, to distinguish general level of intellectual functioning at the two extreme ends of the autism continuum, such judgments are more difficult to render in the case of Kanner autism. It is quite possible that these students possess greater cognitive ability than they may demonstrate, given the intensity of their autistic symptomatology and degree of social isolation. *Bottom Line:* With respect to functioning level judgments, *formal tests scores should be viewed*  Bottom line

with extreme caution for these students, and to a certain extent, for *all* students on the spectrum, as well. Moreover, formal test results should always be *supplemented by informal, context-rich observational data,* since the latter may more accurately reflect the student's ability. Finally, a good rule of thumb to follow regarding intellectual functioning is: *Make no assumptions!*

The next four chapters cover each of the four main areas of functioning which diagnosticians look to when making the diagnosis of autism and related conditions: social behavior; communication and language; interests / activities and imagination; and response to sensation. The fifth chapter addresses the cognitive and social-cognitive deficits that further complicate the diagnostic picture in ASD. It is important to keep the autism spectrum disorders continuum in mind as you read, since a student's placement on the continuum (i.e., diagnostic category) can provide useful information regarding variations both in degree of deficit and symptomatology. Finally, the other crucial piece of information to keep in mind as you traverse the following pages is that autism spectrum disorders are *neurologically*, rather than psychologically or environmentally based.

Take Home Message

- *Autism exists on a continuum* from mild to moderate to severe.

- *Autism is a spectrum disorder* which incorporates varied but similar conditions.

- The term *autism spectrum disorder (ASD) encompasses the entire continuum.*

- Autism can and does exist *with* and *without* mental retardation.

- *Make careful observations*, not assumptions, particularly when judging ability level.

- Autism spectrum disorders are *neurological,* not psychological or environmental.

Chapter Two

Getting to Know Your Student
Atypicalities in Social Understanding and Expression

I chose the word *atypicalities* with great care, for the word allows for *bidirectionality*; that is, it can refer as easily to "deficits" in social behavior (i.e., paucity) as it does to excesses (i.e., overdoing). From this perspective, it can truly be said that *all students with autism spectrum disorders, regardless of level of functioning or specific diagnostic label on the continuum, have difficulty with social behavior.* A couple of examples may serve to clarify this point. Aloof children with Kanner autism typify individuals who evidence a *paucity* of social behavior, whereas children with Asperger syndrome typify *socially excessive* behavior when, unmindful of their listeners' social distress signals, they nevertheless continue to talk "non-stop" about subjects of intense, unilateral interest to them. Both types of students demonstrate atypicalities in social behavior, albeit at different ends of the social continuum.

> Bidirectionality and the two-way street phenomenon

It is also important to recognize that difficulty with social behavior exists on a *receptive* as well as an *expressive* basis. In fact, difficulty with social expression is often a function of the student's lack of understanding of social information. For example, it should be obvious that if one does not understand a social situation, it would be difficult, if not impossible, to generate a skilled social response to it. In this regard, *social behavior—like communication—is indeed a two-way street.* To summarize, it is important to consider social atypicalities from a *bidirectional* perspective, for it is a common misconception to recognize as problematic *only* those instances in which social behavior and/or interest is lacking.

The Plight of the Student with Asperger Syndrome

As noted in the example above, there are some individuals on the autism spectrum who "err" in the other direction, so to speak; that is, they appear highly social (i.e., social-seeking), particularly with respect to items of interest to them—a scenario that is particularly true for those with Asperger syndrome. Notwithstanding, the social overtures of these students are notoriously *one-sided* and can be overbearing, particularly if the listener lacks interest in the subject, or needs to take leave of the situation. Such behavior—though social in the broadest sense of the term—is nonetheless atypical, for *appropriate social behavior is marked by reciprocity (i.e., give and take), and the monitoring of listener needs* so that accommodations may be made.

If the truth be known, students with Asperger syndrome have the toughest "row to hoe" on the autism spectrum, for their one-sided, imposing social overtures and seemingly endless monologues are often deemed self-centered and rude by unknowledgeable caregivers. This is most unfortunate and consummately unfair, for rudeness implies knowledge of what is socially acceptable, and a conscious decision to disregard it. *In Asperger syndrome, as in the other conditions along the continuum, such knowledge is lacking. Bottom Line*: Don't fall prey to the *My Fair Lady* phenomenon, in which Professor Henry Higgans successfully coaches the unpolished Eliza Doolittle into a social paragon of which even Amy Vanderbilt would have been proud. Know instead that *the social anomalies of even the most "social" people on the autism continuum are not merely cosmetic (i.e., skin deep) as in the case of Eliza, but rather deeply rooted and far-reaching.*

 Bottom line

Take Home Message

- There is *always* a problem in social behavior in autism spectrum disorders.

- *Atypicalities in social behavior are bidirectional*, and may take the form of *"deficits"* (i.e., lack of social interest and/or socially motivated behavior), or *excesses* (i.e., one-sided, nonreciprocating approach behavior).

- Problems in social behavior affect the student's ability to *understand* a social situation, and hence to generate a skilled (i.e., appropriate) social *response* to it.

- *Social understanding* is the basis for appropriate *social expression*.

- Students with Asperger syndrome are more likely to manifest symptomatology marked by *social excess*.

- *Students with ASD are not rude!*

Chapter Three

Getting to Know Your Student Impairments in Communication and Language

Communication and *language* represent two interrelated but distinct entities. They will be described in more detail shortly, since impairments in communication and language are among the most misunderstood autistic symptomatology. But first, a few important points about the autism spectrum disorders continuum are in order. To begin with, there is a great deal of variability with respect to communication and language impairment in ASD. Those individuals who are considered less able obviously have the most difficulty. Some are nonverbal, while others are only minimally verbal. In the latter case, these students may be able to understand and express only the most basic information (i.e., that which is related to satisfying their own needs). This is known as communicating for *instrumental* purposes.

The variability in communication and language impairment

At the more able end of the autism spectrum continuum, however, one finds individuals who often *appear* to understand and use language at a rather high level. In fact, individuals with Asperger syndrome are thought by many to have *normal* language. This, however, is *not* the case. Thus, it is important to note that even though students with AS may appear to have *superficially* normal language expression (in terms of grammar and syntax), and even though they may evidence advanced vocabulary usage, they nevertheless manifest difficulty in *social communication*—that is, in the *comprehension and use of language for the purposes of receiving and sending messages.* This aspect of language is known as *pragmatics,* and will be discussed at greater length later in this chapter. This point cannot be over-emphasized, for one of the most common errors made by well-intentioned paras and other caregivers—blinded by the strengths of these individuals—is to *overstate* their abilities in the area of communication and language, and to *assume* competence where none exists. When this occurs, subtle problems in language comprehension and expression are missed, as is the need for communication and language therapy. *Bottom Line*: There is *always* a problem in the *use* of language for social communication (i.e., pragmatics) regardless of the student's level of functioning or particular type of pervasive developmental disorder. Moreover, such problems at the higher levels of functioning may be more insidious, given their subtlety. Worse yet, they may be perceived as *behavioral,* rather than *communicative,* in nature.

 Bottom line

Communication and Language: Different Facets of a Multifaceted Skill

In order to more fully comprehend the interplay between communication and language, and to recognize the type of difficulty that occurs in ASD, it is important to understand the differences between the two terms. Generally speaking, *communication* is the more encompassing term, taking into account not only verbal behavior but, in fact, *all* behavior whether or not there is communicative intent (i.e., a conscious intention on the part of the individual to communicate). For example, the notorious "dirty look" sends a powerful message even if the "sender" tries to suppress it. Similarly, pounding the table with a fist signals frustration in much the same way that raising the arms with fists clenched at a football game signals triumph. Note that *neither message involves the use of words.*

First Things First

It is critically important to bear in mind that *communication always comes first—before language develops.* For example, the cry of a newborn baby signals the parent that the baby needs attention. Importantly, even though the crying has message value (i.e., alerts the parent to check on the infant), it is nonetheless uttered *without* communicative intent on the infant's part. *The intent to communicate comes much later—* in typical babies at about eight or nine months of age—at the time when parents recognize what they call their baby's "spoiled" cry—his or her conscious *intention* to obtain their attention.

At this juncture it is important to state that even though a child with an autism spectrum disorder manifests an atypical developmental pattern, *it is not so atypical as to reverse the entire process of communication and language development!* In other words, *communication always develops before language, even in individuals with ASD.* Problems occur when well meaning, though misinformed paras and other caregivers try to reverse the process by stressing language *at the expense of communication.* For example, this can occur when an adult interprets the student's nonverbal behavior as a request for something (e.g., food), and yet withholds the desired item in service to the all-too-familiar phrase, *"Use your words."* The point here is that even if students have the words they need in their lexicons, we cannot assume that they know how to *use* them to obtain what they want, because communication and language—though intimately related— nevertheless represent *different* entities. It would be more helpful for the caregiver to elaborate, and hence validate and scaffold the nonverbal message by mapping language on to it; that is, by *supplying the words needed in the context of the nonverbal request*—a practice that facilitates *both* comprehension and expression.

Honor the student's communicative attempts

Similarly, insisting on the full sentence, particularly from students who are not yet at the multi-word utterance stage, can be counterproductive. Not only can it cause anxiety and frustration in the student—*both of which may be expressed behaviorally*—it can also create unnecessary layers of excess verbiage between the child's utterance and the adult's response. Consider for example, the student who has just learned to combine two-to-three word phrases. If s/he requests, *"more cookie,"* it would be a mistake to withhold the cookie until the child has been *prompted* to say, *"I want more cookie please,"* since the latter is above the child's customary two-to-three word utterance stage. Besides, there are other ways to elaborate on responses that are not only more consistent with the child's ability, but also more natural, as well. For example, the caregiver can pretend not to understand (known colloquially as "playing dumb") when the child says, *"more cookie,"* asking, *"Who wants more cookie?"* This gives the student the opportunity to elaborate upon his/her response, and to practice two important communicative functions: to *answer* a question and to make a *request.* More importantly, it also enables the student to engage in a *context-driven social interaction*, as opposed to the mere repetition of a *prompted* longer utterance. *Bottom Line:* The *"use your words"* and *"full sentence press"* scenarios, though common markers along the educational landscape for individuals with autism spectrum disorders, are better left unsaid in favor of more *natural* means of facilitating language use. This brings us to the much taken-for-granted concept of *language.*

☀ Bottom line

In his book *Seeing Voices*, Oliver Sacks described language as "the symbolic currency for the exchange of meaning." This is an apt description of language, since it emphasizes two important features. The first is that language is *symbolic*; that is, words are symbols that stand for things. Further, symbols may be verbal or nonverbal. For example, the word *snow* means frozen white stuff to us, whether or not the word is spoken, read, or rendered in sign language. Moreover, the word *snow* would still carry the same meaning whether or not we experience snow each winter or live in the tropics without it. That's the beauty of symbols. When we *understand* their agreed-upon meanings, we can *use* them to express our thoughts and ideas about things that are not necessarily present at the time. Conversely, *when we don't understand what the words mean, we can't use them effectively.* This point, though obvious, is one that is often missed in ASD.

Comprehension: The Foundation for Meaningful Expression

The second feature of Sacks' definition—*"the exchange of meaning"*—relates to the highest and most important purpose of language: *that we use it meaningfully to exchange thoughts and ideas with others.* In order to do this we must first *comprehend* what the symbols (e.g., words, manual signs, pictures, etc.) mean. Consequently, in the same way that communication comes *before* language, so too *compre-*

hension comes before meaningful expression. The key concept here is expressed by the word *meaningful*, for it is indeed possible to speak without meaning. The use of *echolalia* for self-stimulatory purposes by some children with autism is indeed the *meaningless* repetition of words heard, but not understood. This brings us to another *Bottom Line*: 1) Don't be dazzled by the spoken word and *assume* comprehension; and 2) Know that in order for words to be used *meaningfully* they must first be understood by the child. This brings us full circle—back to communication.

 Bottom line

Pragmatics: The Glue that Binds Communication and Language

Communication is governed by a feature known as *pragmatics*. Basically, pragmatics refers to the *use* of language in a communicative context. Hence, communication and language come together in the arena of pragmatics. It is important to recognize that of all the features of language, *it is the pragmatic elements that are the most impaired in autism spectrum disorders*.

Table 1 outlines three areas of pragmatic knowledge. The first has to do with the reasons why people speak. For example, people speak to request things, to obtain attention, to express displeasure, and so forth. These are just a few of the pragmatic functions of communication.

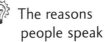 The reasons people speak

Table 1

Three Crucial Areas of Pragmatic Knowledge

1. The ability to employ speech acts to express intentionality in order to accomplish a given purpose (i.e., function)

2. The ability to make judgments (i.e., presuppositions) about the listener's needs and capabilities, in order to regulate speech style and content vis-à-vis listener and/or situational needs

3. The ability to apply the rules of discourse in order to engage in cooperative conversational exchanges

Table 2 not only lists some of the more common pragmatic functions, but also gives examples of how they might be expressed by both verbal and nonverbal individuals with autism spectrum disorders. Moreover, *Mode of Expression* is further broken down into the categories of *prelanguage* and *language* behavior to distinguish between symbolic and non-symbolic expression.

Students with ASD often express these communicative functions *behaviorally*, rather than verbally. This is especially true for those who are nonverbal or who function at the less able end of the autism spectrum continuum. For example, a nonverbal or minimally verbal student with autism who wants something that s/he sees, is likely to simply take it. This is often construed as "stealing" when, in fact, it is the student's attempt to make something happen in the only way s/he knows. Likewise, lacking an appropriate "protest function" (i.e., being able to appropriately refuse or reject something), a student with autism might have no other recourse than to protest *behaviorally*. For example, students who find glue on their fingers aversive (in much the same way as we interpret fingernails scratching on a chalkboard as aversive), are likely to react to the experience by sweeping the pesky art project off their desks. It should be obvious that what looks like a *behavioral* issue on the surface is actually a *communication* issue; that is, *the students' inability to express themselves in more communicatively appropriate (i.e., conventional) ways.*

 The judgments speakers make

Returning to Table 1, the second area of pragmatics listed has to do with the judgments that people make about their listeners' needs. These judgments, called *presuppositions,* enable speakers to know what the listener needs to know in order to understand the message. For example, typical speakers would recognize that the out-of-context utterance, *"That was really something!"* would be indecipherable to a listener without additional information. People with ASD, however, have a great deal of difficulty knowing what the listener needs to know. Consequently, like the example given, they might start in the middle of a thought or idea, failing to provide the background information needed to ground the listener with respect to meaning. In addition, people with ASD also *fail to regulate the style or content of their speech to fit the sit-*

Table 2

PRAGMATIC FUNCTION (Communicative Intent)	FORM (Mode of Expression)	
	Prelanguage Behavior	Language Behavior
REQUEST	Motoric: pulls mom to cookie jar Gestural: points to trampoline	Signs or says, "cookie" Signs or say, "jump"
ACCESS/OBTAIN ATTENTION	Motoric: taps adult's arm Vocal: persistent vocalization Gestural: waving to obtain attention	Signs or says, "Mom" Same as above Same as above
PROTEST/REJECT/REFUSE	Motoric: pushes person away Gestural: shakes head "no" in response to "Do you want toilet?"	Signs or says, "go" Signs or says, "no"
COMMENT/LABEL	Motoric: extends object to show it Gestural: "gestures" dish away at end of snack	Signs or says, "look" or "truck" Signs or says, "finished"; "all done"
OFFER/GIVE	Motoric: extends object to give it Gestural: points to object to indicate person may have it	Signs or says, "here" Signs or says, "take"
ANSWER REPLY/ACKNOWLEDGE	Motoric: crying in response to question Gestural: responds to question via pointing to object; shaking head in response to "want to play?"	Signs or says, "yes" or "no" Same as above
INFORMS/GIVES INFORMATION	Motoric: pulls Mom to broken toy Gestural/vocal: vocalizes while pointing to child crying	Signs or says, "break" Signs or says, "crying"; "baby cry"
SEEKS INFORMATION	Motoric: brings Mom to garage hunches shoulders Vocal: vocalizes with persistent, rising intonation while searching for Mom Gestural: hunches shoulders	Signs or says, "car?" with rising inflection to indicate "where' car?" Signs or says, "Mommy?" with rising inflection to indicate "where's Mom?" Signs or says, "I don't know"
EXPRESSES FEELINGS/EMOTIONAL STATE	Motoric: puts Mom's hand on face to indicate "hot" Gestural: points to scrape on leg	Signs or says, "hot" Signs or says, "hurt"; "boo boo"
GREETING/SOCIAL ROUTINE	Motoric: touches/clings to adult when leaving or greeting Gestural: child waves to adult when leaving or greeting	Signs or says, "good bye", "hi" Same as above
OTHER: **Direct; order; warn; tease; convey humor; exclaim, etc.**	**Formula For Inferring Communicative Intent** 1. Observe the nonverbal or verbal behavior with respect to context 2. Determine whether the response mode is motoric, gestural, or symbolic (manual signs/verbal) 3. Assign a function/intent to the behavior, based upon a "best guess" strategy 4. Evaluate with respect to context	

Based upon the work of: Dore, J. (1974). A pragmatic description of early language development. *Journal of Psycholinguistic Research. 4,* 343-350
Roth, F. P. & Spekman, N. J. (1984). Assessing the pragmatic abilities of children: Part 1. Organizational framework and assessment parameters. *Journal of Speech and Hearing Disorders, 49,* 2-11.

uation, for this too is based on presuppositional knowledge. Consequently, a young man with ASD might speak in the *same* manner to a toddler, as to an adult in authority, as to his mother or father. Typical speakers know that they would need to modulate their vocal delivery, and/or choice of words, to suit both the situation and the particular listener.

The third feature of pragmatics listed in Table 1 concerns the conversational maxims (i.e., rules) which speakers apply when they converse with others. These maxims, common to *all* speakers, can provide useful information when applied to more able students, since the latter already possess a language system, albeit one marked by some degree of deviance.

 The rules of conversation

Table 3 contains the *Four Maxims of Conversational Interaction*, as well as examples of how persons with ASD might violate each of them. The first conversational rule is that of *quantity*. Saying too much or too little violates the rule of quantity. The second rule concerns *quality*. This rule relates to the truth value of the utterance. Erroneous information, whether intentional as in *lying*, or unintentional as in *confabulating* (i.e., relating an untruth that the speaker nonetheless *believes* to be true), interferes with the quality of an utterance. The third conversational rule is that of *relevance*. In order to fulfill this rule, one must stick to the topic under discussion. Tangential comments would violate this maxim. The fourth rule relates to the *clarity* of an utterance. This one is more comprehensive than the previous rules in that it requires a speaker to do all that is necessary to present one's message in a manner that is clear and understandable to the listener. These maxims can provide a useful yardstick for caregivers to use in determining the particular kinds of pragmatic difficulties their students manifest. Such knowledge can enable you to become a more informed, and hence helpful, communicative partner.

The Communication-Behavior Connection

To summarize, impairments in communication and language, though considered hallmark features of autism spectrum disorders, are nonetheless often misinterpreted and misunderstood. This is understandable, since most of us learn to use language so early in life that we don't remember how we

Table 3

The Four Maxims of Conversational Interaction

Maxim One: **Quantity**—the rule to be informative without being verbose. Speaking "non-stop" without regard to "social distress" signals is an example of difficulty with *quantity.*

Maxim Two: **Quality**—the rule to be truthful. Confabulation (i.e., filling in knowledge gaps with false information that the speaker *believes* to be true) is an example of difficulty with *quality.*

Maxim Three: **Relevance**—the rule to contribute only information that is pertinent to the topic and situation. Tangential comments constitute difficulty with the rule of *relevance.*

Maxim Four: **Clarity**—the rule that the information conveyed is clear and understandable to the listener. Initiating a conversation in the middle of a thought, without providing background information, is an example of a problem with the rule of *clarity.*

Based upon the work of Grice, 1975

Twachtman, D.D. (Summer, 1996). There's a lot more to communication than talking! *The Morning News.* Jenison Public Schools, Jenison, MI. Reprinted with permission.

learned it or ever having been without it, for that matter. As such, it is easy to take the ability to comprehend and express information for granted, since most people perform these functions effortlessly. In reality, *the ability to comprehend and use language is the most complex skill that human beings are called upon to develop.* It is indeed understandable then that individuals with autism spectrum disorders have difficulty with many of the facets of this multifaceted skill. Further, the particular type and degree of difficulty will *vary* considerably among students. For those at the lower end of the continuum the deficits are more severe, and hence more obvious. For those at the more able end of the continuum the deficits are far more subtle, causing these students to *appear* even more able than they actually are!

A final word is in order before turning to the next area of functioning affected in autism. Because communication is indeed a two-way street, the problems in communication and language evidenced by individuals with ASD are often exacerbated by well-intentioned, though unknowledgeable paras and other caregivers. This can take many different forms, the most common of which are *assuming communicative competence where little to none exists, and/or mistaking problems in communication for problems in behavior.* Both of these misjudgments constitute serious roadblocks in the education of students with these conditions. Despite their significance, these misconceptions are easily remedied through increased knowledge and understanding of not only autism spectrum disorders, but also of the individual variations in the students who manifest them. Thus, while the amount of information in this chapter is far more detailed than will be seen in other chapters, it is felt to be crucially important to the educational well being of students with ASD. Hopefully, it will serve to soften the message which is the hardest sell in autism, that:

All behavior communicates. Hence, what may *appear* to be an act of willful noncompliance, may be, in actuality, the student's *idiosyncratic* attempt to send a message that s/he is unable to get across in any other more *conventional* way. Moreover, since it is the caregiver's judgments that determine how the student will be perceived, *what the caregiver does not know can, and often does, jeopardize the student's learning.*

Roadblocks to success

Take Home Message

- *There is always a problem in the use of language for social communication purposes (i.e., pragmatics),* regardless of the student's level of functioning or type of pervasive developmental disorder.

- *It is common to be blinded by the strengths of more able students,* and hence attribute to them a higher level of communicative competence than exists.

- *Communication always develops before language,* even in individuals with ASD.

- Insisting on longer and longer utterances *before* the student is developmentally ready to produce them may produce anxiety and frustration.

- *Comprehension precedes meaningful expression,* but it should never be merely *assumed.*

- *Students with ASD have difficulty with all three areas of pragmatics:* the *functions* of communication (e.g., requesting, protesting, etc.); making *social judgments* by which to regulate the flow of information; and understanding and abiding by *conversational rules.*

- Two of the most common caregiver errors in ASD are *assuming communicative competence,* and *mistaking problems in communication for problems in behavior.*

- *All* behavior communicates!

Chapter Four

Getting to Know Your Student
Restricted Repertoire of Interests and Activities; Problems With Imagination

Circumscribed (i.e., narrow and restricted), is a word that defines both the interests and scope of activities preferred by individuals with autism spectrum disorders. Unlike neurotypical children, whose expansive interests suggest an almost fickle "Jack of all trades" quality, those with autism and related conditions demonstrate a far narrower range of interests, concomitant with a restricted repertoire of activities. Likewise, students with ASD are also known for their preference for sameness—a feature that dovetails well with their above-noted limited interests and activities. A few examples may serve to clarify the differences between neurotypical children and those with ASD.

Uncommon and Restricted Interests and Activities

Anyone who has watched typically developing children at recess can attest to their wide-ranging interests in the realm of playground equipment, games and activities, and even each other. Enter onto that same recess scene a young boy with autism, and you will likely see a child, who is both literally and figuratively, on the periphery; that is, on the perimeter of the playground, and most definitely on the outskirts of the playful social scene. Similarly, consider the adolescent boy with Asperger syndrome whose fascination with weather phenomena overshadows all other interests (not to mention academic pursuits), or the little girl with classic autism who is contented to sit for hours lining up different colored blocks. All of these students evidence the restricted repertoire of interests and activities commonly seen in ASD. Moreover, these children demonstrate little or no interest in the wide variety of toys and games which neurotypical children regularly seek out and enjoy—a lack of interest which negatively impacts their ability to benefit from the concept-building opportunities that these activities and toys provide.

The examples given above concern interests that are relatively conventional. It should be noted, however, that the interests of students with ASD are often quite unusual, if not downright peculiar. To wit, some children are fascinated by beams of light, evidencing little interest in anything else, while others give inordinate amounts of time and attention to twirling string, flicking objects, or tossing sand or water in the air. There are many reasons why individuals with ASD evidence narrow bands of interest and activity. Some relate to sensory issues, and will be discussed in the next chapter. A consideration of others is beyond this manual's scope. Even so, regardless of the reasons for their narrow bands of activity and interest, and the sameness which these solitary pursuits afford them, such interests nonetheless serve a "gating" function; that is, by absorbing the student's interest and attention, they help to "hold at bay" the stimulating effects of a fast-paced, transient, and inexplicable social world.

There are two important things that paras and other caregivers need to keep in mind. First, *individuals with autism have no control over their interests,* any more than neurotypical people do. The difference is that the latter individuals can be enticed into attending to things which do not interest them if the consequences matter enough to them. For example, a neurotypical little boy may have as little interest in school work as his classmate with autism. But unlike the latter, recess may be the "hook" to motivate him. Similarly, the class "social butterfly" may be prevailed upon to work harder than she wants to if the teacher threatens that she may not pass on to the next grade with her friends. *Such socially mediated strategies do little to motivate students with ASD,* given their lack of interest in these kinds of consequences. What we, as caregivers need to do is find creative ways to use the students' often arcane interests to motivate them. For example, the little boy with Asperger syndrome may be prevailed upon to finish his math work if the "hook" to motivate him is granting him 5 minutes to talk about a topic of intense interest to him. Do remember, however, that your part of the "bargain" is that *you need to listen*!

In search of educational "hooks"

The second thing that paras and other caregivers need to keep uppermost in their minds is that the restricted repertoire of interests and activities demonstrated by students with ASD is not only *devoid of conscious or willful decision making,* it is in fact, a *symptom* of their disorder over which they have little or no control. Consequently, if and when these students *resist* school activities—whether academic or social—they should not be summarily "punished" for their resistance. It would be far more productive to *entice* their participation by using their narrow interests first as a *hook*, and later as a *bridge* to more expansive educational pursuits. We do this for neurotypical children. The principles are the same here, even if the interests are different. For a neurotypical child, recess may be the hook. For one with ASD, it might be time spent on an arcane topic of interest, as in the example cited above.

An *Imaginative* Look at Imagination

Imagination is a construct about which there is much confusion in ASD, and with good reason, for it "plays out" differently depending upon the particular type of pervasive developmental disorder manifested by the student. Let's start with something we can all agree on, given its logical basis. *Students at the less able end of the autism spectrum continuum have significant impairments in the ability to engage in imaginative activities.* Conventional wisdom certainly supports this view. Less able children do not have the capacity to suspend reality and go into the *"as if"* mode required for imaginary thinking.

Children who are more able may demonstrate the rudiments of imagination, but they rarely develop these into play sequences which build upon one another. For example, these children may be able to give the doll a bottle, but may not be able to expand upon the activity or build a play scenario around it. Moreover, their impoverished imaginative play tends to be repetitive, giving the impression that they are stuck, with little idea of what to do next to extend and elaborate the play sequence.

 Don't be fooled by superficial rudiments of play behavior

Unless one observes these children for an extended period of time, it is easy to be *misled* by the superficial rudiments of the type of imaginative behavior represented by such activities as feeding a doll or stirring a pot. *Extended observation, however, often reveals that their play is quite restricted and repetitive.* In addition, children with ASD can also "fool" the casual onlooker into thinking that they are more capable than they actually are, particularly when they exhibit isolated play skills they may have been taught. Unfortunately, though superficially impressive, these play skills have little depth.

Difficulties in imagination may be more difficult to detect in older students, since opportunities for play diminish as students approach the middle and high school years. Moreover, as the child gets older, problems in imagination may be manifested in different and more subtle ways. I am reminded of Jason, an 11-year-old boy with Asperger syndrome who for an art project was asked to combine parts of three real animals that he had readily drawn (e.g., a dog, a cat, and a horse), to create an *imaginary* animal. Jason responded to this assignment with great distress, saying over and over again, "But it doesn't exist!" Jason's art teacher thought the problem was one of noncompliance. In reality, the problem stemmed from Jason's inability to *imagine* an animal that did not already exist in the world; hence, his inability to *create* one.

The "Outer Limits" of Imagination

Individuals with Asperger syndrome, in particular, present the greatest challenge to one's understanding of the concept of imagination, since most people view imagination as *lacking* in ASD. In reality, some (but not all) students with Asperger syndrome actually seem to have *too much* imagination. And as the old adage goes, "too much of a good thing is not necessarily a good thing!" *Sometimes these children have significant difficulty in distinguishing fact (i.e., reality) from fanta-*

 Too much of a good thing...

sy. For example, I once provided consultation services for an 8-year-old boy with Asperger syndrome who tried to hang himself on a coat hook by his collar, because he had seen the burglars in the movie, *Home Alone* do that—*without ill effects*—to Kevin, the little boy in the film. In this case, it is easy to see that *too much imagination, combined with too little social understanding and judgment, can be a recipe for disaster!* It is less obvious, though consummately important to acknowledge, that an uninitiated observer might judge the child's "imaginative" act as his desire to harm himself, thus missing the real reason for the behavior (i.e., *impairment in imagination*), and hence, the opportunity to address it. *Bottom Line: Like atypicalities in social behavior, imagination, too, is bidirectional (i.e., characterized by too much or too little)*. Moreover, as in the case of social excess, it is the individual with Asperger Syndrome whose sense of imagination often spills over into the excessive range.

Before leaving this topic, it is important to note that because play behavior is an area of significant difficulty for students with ASD, *the development of play skills should never be left to chance*. While it is not the responsibility of the para to develop approaches to stimulate imagination and play, it is definitely within their purview to *facilitate* play behaviors and imaginative activities under the direction of certified staff. *Without concentrated attention and facilitation within the context of meaningful activities, play behavior will continue to remain significantly impoverished*. For young children, the ideal time to facilitate play, either by themselves or with neurotypical peers, is during that period of time known as *free play*. For older students recess can provide an appropriate setting. The term *free play*, though appropriate for neurotypical children, is anything but appropriate for children with ASD. A more apt term would be *facilitated play*, to underscore the important role of paras in the development of play skills for students with ASD. *Bottom Line: There is no such thing as free play for students with autism spectrum disorders*. In order for play behavior to occur it must be *set up, facilitated, supported*, and *monitored*. So whatever you do, arrange your coffee break at a less crucial time than that which is devoted to "free" play.

💡 Bottom line

💡 Bottom line

Take Home Message

- Students with ASD demonstrate a *narrow range of interests* that is often *unusual* in nature, and a *restricted repertoire of activities* that reflects their *preference for sameness.*

- These characteristics are not conscious choices, but rather *symptoms* of their disorder.

- Since students with ASD have as little control over their interests as neurotypical students do, *it is up to paras and other caregivers to find "hooks" to entice their interest and participation.*

- When play behavior is present in ASD it tends to be *impoverished.*

- *Atypicalities in imagination, like those in social behavior, are also bidirectional*; that is, imagination may be characterized by *too much*, as can be the case in Asperger syndrome, or *too little*, as in the case of less able children.

- There is no such thing as *free play* for students with ASD!

Chapter Five

Getting to Know Your Student
Abnormal Response to Sensation

In many ways, abnormal response to sensation is the "stepchild symptom" in autism spectrum disorders—undervalued and unappreciated. Yet, the significance of sensory issues is of paramount importance, as the following truisms clearly demonstrate:

• Human beings have no way of experiencing the world other than to take in information through their senses.

• Abnormal *sensory input* equals abnormal *motor output*!

Variations on the Theme of Sensation

There are five senses that are easily recognized: *sight, smell, taste, touch,* and *hearing*. There are also two other senses known as the *"hidden senses."* The first of these is called *proprioception,* and refers to the internal feedback that human beings get from their muscles and joints. This information, though below the level of awareness, enables us to move effortlessly through space. Proprioception works with the other "hidden sense"—known as the *vestibular* sense. Located in the semicircular canals in the inner ear, the vestibular system also gives us important data about the position of our body in space (e.g., whether we are sitting up or lying down).

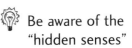 Be aware of the "hidden senses"

The other senses are easier to understand, because their functioning is not below the level of consciousness. For example, it is obvious to all of us that color is experienced through vision, and that music is experienced through the sense of hearing. In fact, we can even *imagine* what an abnormal response to color might be like without actually experiencing it for ourselves, since the concept of color blindness is a common enough phenomenon to permit at least an *intellectual* understanding of it. Likewise, the closely related senses of taste and smell are quite straightforward. Moreover, anyone who has had a cold severe enough to adversely affect these senses also knows how disconcerting abnormal response to sensation can be.

The sense of touch allows us to feel through our skin the things with which we come into contact. The *tactile system*, as it is called, is comprised of three parts: *light touch*, *discriminative touch*, and *pressure/pain*. The first is an alerting system. The second allows us to discriminate differences between things *solely* through touch. For example, people with intact discriminative touch can distinguish between a dime and a nickel in their pockets, without actually having to look at the coins. Pressure / pain allows us not only to register these two obvious sensations, but also to react to temperature variations, as well.

There is a great deal of variability in sensory impairment both within and among individuals with autism spectrum disorders. Short-circuits in the sensory system probably produce the most dramatic effects, and are by far the most difficult to comprehend. For example, it is almost impossible to imagine a sensory system in which color is experienced as *sound*, and music (or sound in general) is experienced as *color*. Notwithstanding, this condition—known as *synesthesia*—not only exists, but has been reported in autism and related conditions.

Behavioral manifestations of sensory anomalies

Most sensory abnormalities in ASD are probably more in the realm of distortions, as opposed to those that are either frankly disordered as in the case of synesthesia, or absent as in the case of blindness or deafness. For example, many students with ASD have visual or auditory perceptual problems. In the former case, their eyes in a very real sense play tricks on them. The child who fails to raise his or her arms to catch a ball until it's too late may have a visual perceptual problem with respect to judging distance. These children may resist physical education and recess activities involving games like

Dodge Ball or *Soccer,* since their visual perceptual problems leave them ill-equipped to deal with the "onslaught" of the rapidly moving ball. In the case of auditory impairments, difficulties have been reported for both the *frequency* (pitch), and *intensity* (loudness) of sounds. For example, I once worked with a child who turned off the fluorescent lights because he perceived the humming sound they emit as too loud. These children can find even conversational tones off-putting, if not aversive.

Disturbances in the sense of touch may be manifested in several different ways. Students with tactile defensiveness are troubled by light touch and by sticky and/or gooey substances on their hands, as noted in the example cited earlier regarding the child who had an adverse reaction to glue. Furthermore, as unlikely as it may seem, children who are put off by *light* touch often crave *deep* touch (i.e., pressure). Thus, a child who finds light touch aversive may react aggressively to someone simply brushing past him or her, while at the same time s/he may nonetheless desire deep pressure sensation. Conventional wisdom won't help here, since the child's over reaction to light touch would lead us to the erroneous conclusion that s/he finds *all* touch aversive. Hence, it is only through the development of knowledge regarding the tactile variability among children with ASD that we can come to understand and acknowledge that *different types of touch are experienced differently both within and among children with ASD.* Even more perplexing is the child's unusual response to pain. For example, it is quite common for children who react defensively to light touch, to actually have *undersensitivity* to pain—exactly the opposite of what you'd expect. These are the children who can take the toughest spills on the playground in stride, and as the saying goes, "pick themselves up, brush themselves off, and start all over again!"

"Deceptive" responses to sensation

Problems in proprioception are even more difficult to grasp. Children who have proprioceptive abnormalities have difficulty judging how much force or pressure to apply when picking something up or when holding on to something. Consequently, they may hug someone too hard, in fact, hard enough to cause discomfort. Similarly, they may hold a pencil too lightly to make marks on a page. Further, abnormalities in proprioception may be responsible, at least in part, for the movement problems one sees in many of the children with autism, and the clumsiness and/or awkwardness associated with Asperger syndrome.

Difficulties in the vestibular system can lead to a phenomenon known as *gravitional insecurity*. Students who experience this type of problem feel secure *only* when their feet are either on the ground or other stable surface. Consequently, these students generally avoid swings and other types of playground equipment which involve leaving the security of the ground. Gravitational insecurity, therefore, interferes with environmental exploration, in general.

Difficulties in the proprioceptive, vestibular, and tactile systems can also create *motor planning problems*. Students with these types of problems may not know how to use various pieces of playground equipment, or may not be able to position their bodies so that they are able to explore an apparatus which interests them. For example, a child with motor planning difficulties may enjoy going down a slide, but may have difficulty sequencing his or her hands and feet in the manner necessary to climb up the ladder. *Bottom Line:* A student's lack of participation or refusal to engage in physical activities may be related to his or her *abnormal response to sensation*, and *not* to noncompliance.

🔖 Bottom line

Things Are Not Always What They Seem

Two additional points are in order. The first is that *students with ASD may manifest one or more sensory issues at the same time*. It should be obvious that the presence of multiple sensory abnormalities has a more pronounced effect upon the student's functioning than does a single sensory issue. The second point—and one which paras and other caregivers need to be especially mindful of—is that *the sensory impairment in ASD has a kind of "on again, off again" quality*. In other words, there are times when sensory issues loom large, and other times when the child manages to take them in stride. This on again, off again quality makes it *appear* as though sensory issues are under the control of the student. But in ASD *things are seldom what they seem*—a maxim that all of you are urged to keep uppermost in your minds when interacting with your students! In the case of sensation, as in so many other aspects of functioning, factors such as *fatigue and anxiety exert a negative effect on the sensory system,* while factors such as *comfort level, motivation, and trust have a positive effect upon one's tolerance for adversity.*

Unfortunately, sensory issues in students with ASD are very often either ignored or given short shrift. In my opinion, this often occurs because they are not recognized as *sensory* issues, but rather judged as *behavioral* ones. This is not to imply that caregivers are callous, but rather to suggest that because sensory perception is a *subjective* experience, judgments about what someone else perceives can be difficult, especially without some rudimentary understanding of the sensory system. This is especially true regarding sensory experiences that are unusual—outside what most people experience—as is often the case in autism. For example, neurotypical people can easily understand that scratching a chalkboard with one's fingernails is off-putting, since most of us react to this experience similarly. (Some of you are probably cringing as you read this!). The important point here is that because we can easily *relate to* this experience, we can more easily *understand* it.

 The sensory-behavioral connection

Consider again the example cited earlier of the child with ASD who is as put off by glue on his/her hands as we are by fingernails scratching on a chalkboard. Since the child's experience is not one that neurotypical people find particularly troublesome, it doesn't "jump out" at us as frankly aversive. Under this circumstance, if the child proceeds to throw the sticky art project off the desk, what we see is the behavior (i.e., *the physical act*), not the motivation behind it (i.e., *the aversive sensory experience*). Hence, in failing to recognize the aversive effect which the glue had on the student, we also fail to recognize that *his/her behavior is motivated by sensory discomfort, rather than noncompliance.* It should be obvious then that when paras and other caregivers lack knowledge of sensory issues, they are more apt to make erroneous judgments regarding the motivation behind specific behaviors. Here again we see that what we *don't* know can indeed adversely affect the student. *Bottom Line:* Learn as much as you can about your particular student's response to sensation, and *always look beyond the external behavior* that you see to determine whether or not there is an *internal, sensory-based*

Bottom line

component to it that you cannot see. Moreover, since issues related to sensation may not be obvious to those of us who have intact sensory systems, it is necessary for paras and other caregivers to be not only *knowledgeable* about the ways in which abnormal response to sensation may be manifested, but also especially *vigilant* regarding activities and environmental occurrences that their students may find off-putting, or worse yet, aversive.

Take Home Message

- Abnormal *sensory input* equals abnormal *motor output*.

- Sensory impairment in ASD can be characterized by *oversensitivity* (e.g., tactile and auditory defensiveness); *undersensitivity* (e.g., absence of pain); or *"short circuits"* (e.g., synesthesia).

- There is *significant variability* with respect to the *number and type* of sensory anomalies, and the *manner* in which they are manifested both among and within students with ASD.

- *Fatigue* and *anxiety* (on the negative side), and *comfort level, motivation*, and *trust* (on the positive side) contribute to the *"on again, off again"* quality of sensory impairment in ASD.

- To avoid erroneously classifying sensory issues as behaviorally-based, *always look beyond the external behavior that you see,* in order to determine whether or not there is an *internal*, sensory-based component to it that you cannot see.

Chapter Six

Getting to Know Your Student
Theory of Mind;
Information Processing;
Executive Function

The complexities (and perplexities!) go on and on in autism spectrum disorders. Add to the four areas of disordered functioning covered in the preceding chapters the problems that occur in the cognitive and social-cognitive constructs of *theory of mind*, *information processing*, and *executive function*, and it becomes obvious why autism spectrum disorders are termed *multifaceted*. My job in the next few pages is to sort out and simplify these additional "facets" so that you can understand how they affect students' understanding and behavior. The goal here is to "scratch the surface," but in an area "fertile" enough to permit understanding and application by those of you in the trenches.

Theory of Mind: Fueling Station for the "If I Were You" Phenomenon

The ability to understand another person's point of view—colloquially speaking, to "step into his or her shoes"—is known generically as *perspective taking*. This skill allows us to understand how a person "feels" (i.e., what his/her thoughts are) about something even if we don't happen to agree with (i.e., share) that person's particular viewpoint. The roots of *empathy* (i.e., sharing in the vicarious experiences of others) are found in, and vary according to one's capacity for perspective taking. Indeed, there is a great deal of variability with respect to both perspective taking and empathy among neurotypical people, a fact which underscores the complexities involved in these processes. Thus, some individuals step into another person's shoes quite easily, while others find it difficult to make the journey from their own frames of reference to those of others. Because *our ability to take the perspectives of students with ASD is crucial to understanding their needs and rendering appropriate educational care,* it is important to examine the capricious nature of this distinctly human ability. The following example addresses a perspective taking minefield to which most people can easily relate.

Consider this: You are late for a very important appointment. You pull your car out into the passing lane only to get behind a car going slower than the posted speed limit. You "tolerate" the situation briefly, in fact only for about as long as you hold out any hope that the driver will pull over to let you pass. When it becomes excruciatingly obvious that that isn't going to happen, you will probably do any one of the following: lean on the horn, flash your headlights, and say (or at least think) a few unmentionable words. (The worst perspective takers probably enter "road rage" at this point!). Now consider this: It's one week later, and you're the driver in the lead car. You look in your rear view mirror and see someone driving much too close. Chances are, you have a few unkind thoughts of your own at this point for the "rude" driver "sitting on your bumper." Moral of story: *Your perspective changes depending upon your particular vantage point*—in this case, whether you're looking out of the windshield or in the rear view mirror!

This example serves to illustrate a few important points about perspective taking:

- Generally speaking, perspective taking is *inversely* proportional to one's degree of emotional involvement. In other words, *the more emotionally vested you are in your own position, the less able you are to understand another person's point of view.*

- Perspective taking is often situation dependent (i.e., *perspectives vary as situations vary).*

- The ability to take perspective *decreases* as anxiety and stress *increase.*

- Perspective taking requires the establishment of *a link*

Perspective taking difficulty is a shared phenomenon

between observed physical behavior (e.g., driving too slowly, or following too closely), *and perceived mental state* (e.g., inconsiderateness).

- Perspective taking difficulty is a *shared* phenomenon; hence, *our* ability to take the perspective of the student with ASD is an *essential* part of care giving.

Theory of mind (ToM) may be thought of as the "governing body" of perspective taking. Uta Frith, in her book, *Autism: Explaining the Enigma,* defines ToM as "the ability to predict relationships between *external states of affairs* and *internal states of mind*" [emphasis supplied]. Simon Baron-Cohen, a well-respected researcher, refers to this phenomenon as *"mentalizing."* The latter enables us to figure out behavior by attributing mental states to people. Neurotypical people do this all the time, as a way of making sense out of circumstances and events. *Individuals with ASD have significant difficulty doing this.* The italicized words in each of the following examples are familiar mental state terms that people regularly use in making sense of another person's actions: She *thinks* she's so smart; he *knows* he's in trouble; she *believes* she'll win; and he *feels* cheated. Note that in each case the observer makes an *inference* based upon the behavior that s/he sees. Two important points are in order: 1) *Inferences are educated guesses which may or may not be correct*; and 2) *Inferences link thought (mental) to action (physical), thereby enabling one to understand (i.e., make sense of) a situation or event.*

Linking external behavior with mental state

Theory of Mind and Neurotypical Behavior

An example may help to clarify how an intact theory of mind helps neurotypical people to understand the world, and in the case of ASD, how impairment in this ability interferes with such understanding. An 8-year-old, neurotypical boy walks into the kitchen to ask his mother for a cookie. He sees her talking angrily to someone on the telephone. She looks up, sees her son as she slams the phone down, and asks harshly, *"What is it now?"* Being theory-of-mind-savvy, the child will probably abort his cookie mission, since his *observation of his mother's external behavior* would cause him to *infer her angry*

☼ Using prediction
as a guideline for
behavior

mental state, and consequently to *predict that she will refuse his request.* In other words, his intact ToM mechanism allows him to *"size up the situation,"* (something neurotypical people do on a regular basis), *and use that information as a guideline for modifying his behavior.* Consequently, concluding that his mother probably won't acquiesce to his request for a cookie, he decides not to ask for one. On the other hand, his 10-year-old brother with moderate autism—and the ToM deficits that interfere with his recognition of the links between *external behavior* and *internal motivation*—would likely not only ask for a cookie, but would also be at-a-loss to understand his mother's negative response!

☼ Three aspects of
theory of mind

While the concept of theory of mind is quite complex, the three most important aspects of it which paras and other caregivers need to keep in mind are contained in Table 4. Essentially, having an intact theory of mind enables an individual to *infer* how another person might think or feel based upon that person's *external behavior.* In the cookie example above, the mother's behavior is linked to her mood. These inferences, if they are reasonable, enable one to make sense of activities and events so that predictions regarding behavior may be made. Recognizing his mother's "bad mood," the 8-year-old boy *predicts* that his mother will probably refuse his request for a cookie. Finally, the individual uses the information to make the *modifications* and *adjustments* in his/her behavior. The little boy decides not to ask for a cookie.

Table 4

Components of Theory of Mind
Step 1 Inferring a person's internal mental state based upon the external behavior that s/he exhibits
Step 2 Predicting future behavior based upon one's inferences regarding mental state
Step 3 Modifying/adjusting one's own behavior, based upon the judgments made

It is important to keep in mind that the type of thinking that is required in theory of mind activities, though second nature to neurotypical people, is one that is *significantly impaired* in students with ASD. There are two main reasons for this. For one thing, students with ASD have difficulty dealing with ambiguities and nuances (i.e., shades of gray), preferring the comfort zone which a "black or white" perspective affords them. For another, they have difficulty with the critical thinking skills involved in making inferences and predictions, both of which are crucial to ToM.

Theory of Mind and Autism Spectrum Disorders

As in all autistic symptomatology, there is a great deal of variability in ToM among those on the autism spectrum continuum. Less able individuals and very young children have significant theory of mind issues. Not only do they fail to recognize another person's specific point of view, they also fail to recognize that other people actually have viewpoints that are separate and apart from their own. According to Charles Hart, for these students it is as if the mind is like a *universal* computer to which everyone has his or her own terminal. Consequently, if there is something on the (universal) mind, it is theoretically on "everyone's mind."

Hart, author and parent of a son with high-functioning autism, tells a revealing story to illustrate how he arrived at this conclusion. One day when his son was approximately 14 years of age he was sitting across the room from his father reading a book. When he came to a word that he did not understand, he pointed to it and said—*well outside of his father's visual range*—*"What's this word, Dad?"* A typical 14-year-old young man would know that he would have to *show* his father the printed word in order for him to see it. He would also know that without doing so, their experiences with respect to the printed word would be *different*. The young man in the above-noted example, however, did not recognize the need to show the word to his father, due to his theory of mind deficits. Based upon the boy's behavior, one might hypothesize the following: Since the word was in his "mind's eye" view, he assumed it was in his father's as well, since to

The consequences of *assuming* a shared perspective

his way of thinking, the mind is universal, *not separate and distinct*. Stated differently, his deficits in theory of mind led him to erroneously conclude that he and his father shared the *same* experience, and hence, the *same* knowledge base.

Deficits in ToM which engender this type of thinking are often behind the explosive behavior which some students exhibit if their needs—*as they perceive them*—are not met; that is, they assume that our experience is the same as theirs. Hence, they are at-a-loss to understand our lack of responsiveness. Likewise, ToM deficits are also involved in presuppositional difficulty, for, in perceiving experiences to be "universal," the individual would see no need to ground the listener vis-à-vis the subject. It is easy to see how a lack of knowledge regarding the contribution of ToM deficits to the student's behavior would lead caregivers to misconstrue the motivation behind the student's response.

Theory of Mind and Empathy

It should be obvious that the ability to engage in empathic behavior—a more affectively-based perspective taking task— would also either be lacking or severely limited in students who evidence overall difficulty with perspective taking. Hence, students with ASD who show no remorse for causing their classmates discomfort will likely be reprimanded for their "insensitivity," as though their behavior were a matter of choice, rather than a clear demonstration of their inability to step into the shoes of another person and perceive the situation *as if* they themselves were experiencing it. Thus, empathic behavior not only requires *knowledge* that other people experience things differently, but also the ability to *imagine* oneself in the same position—areas of profound difficulty in ASD. *Bottom Line:* Exercise extreme caution in making judgments about what students with autism spectrum disorders both *perceive* and hence *respond* to with respect to their perceptions.

 Bottom line

Theory of Mind and Asperger Syndrome

It is important to note that while theory of mind deficits exist for *all* those who are on the autism spectrum continuum, students with Asperger syndrome are thought by some professionals to have somewhat greater ability in this area than those with autism. In my own experience, I have found this to be true for some adolescents and older students with AS. For example, using a variation on a classic theory of mind experiment (i.e., the *Smarties* task), I showed a young boy with Asperger syndrome a *Crest Toothpaste* box and asked him to guess what was inside it. He guessed, *"Toothpaste."* I then opened the box and revealed that, instead of toothpaste, there were pencils inside. Next, I told him that I was going to invite his mother into the room and asked, *"What do you think she will think is in the box?"* Unable to separate what was in his mind (*based upon his experience*), from what was in his mother's mind (*lacking such experience*), he said, *"Pencils."* I have also used this task with older students with Asperger syndrome and have achieved different results with some of them; that is, on this rudimentary theory of mind task, some were able to understand that an *unknowledgable* observer would *think* that the box contained toothpaste, given its label (i.e., *Crest)*. Paras and other caregivers are urged not to be fooled by those who "pass" these rudimentary theory of mind "tests." *Bottom Line:* Theory of mind is an extremely complex, multifaceted construct. Even though *some* more able students may evidence understanding of lower-level ToM tasks, *it should not be assumed that they would be able to understand higher-order tasks* such as those involving the perspectives and motivations of others, or those related to what people think about what other people think. The latter is called a *second order* theory of mind task, and is difficult for even the highest functioning individuals with ASD. An example of this is, *"What does Mary think that Sue thinks about the new student?"*

Bottom line

The Theory of Mind—Social Behavior Connection

Before leaving this topic, it is important to consider the specific aspects of theory of mind that are so problematic for students with ASD. For one thing, in order to make inferences regarding mental state, students have to be able to tolerate ambiguity, for as noted above, inferences are nothing more than educated guesses that may or may not be correct. As noted previously, *individuals with ASD are notoriously poor at dealing with nuances and shades of gray, preferring concrete facts to amorphous possibilities.* For another thing, students with ASD also have difficulty with the future orientation of the predictions which serve as the basis for modifying one's own behavior, as well as with the *application* of skills in general. Both of these involve *executive function* ability, an area of acknowledged difficulty and one that will be discussed at length later in this chapter. But the overarching reason why theory of mind tasks are so difficult for students with ASD is that such tasks involve *social understanding and judgment—areas of profound difficulty for even the highest functioning individuals.*

Take Home Message

- Perspective taking is a *shared* phenomenon: Our ability to take the student's perspective is *crucial* to his/her success.

- Students with ASD have significant difficulty with *perspective taking, empathy*, and *theory of mind.*

- Theory of mind deficits in ASD interfere with the student's ability to *size up* a situation.

- Students with ASD have *significant difficulty dealing with the ambiguities involved in making inferences and predictions, and in dealing with nuances,* all of which are required in ToM activities.

- *Theory of mind tasks require social understanding and social judgment—*areas of *profound difficulty* in students with ASD.

Information Processing: Where the Rubber Hits the Road

If schooling could be reduced to its "lowest common denominator" surely it would be that of information; that is, the ultimate purpose of education is to teach students to take in, process, express, and/or otherwise utilize information. This is a tall order for students with autism spectrum disorders, for *current research clearly shows that these students have significant difficulty with information processing.* At the risk of oversimplification, Table 5 contains a schematic to guide you in understanding the highly complex information processing system. Its linear format is somewhat deceptive, since in reality the operations involved in processing information not only occur in split-second time so as to appear simultaneous, they are also *continuous*, *ongoing*, and hence *bidirectional*. Their stepwise linear presentation here is simply a convenience to enable you to more easily understand the components of this complex system.

The first level of information processing is that of *sensation*—the taking in of information through the senses. The next level is that of *perception*—the ability to attach meaning to the information. For example, if you reach into your pocket and feel a long, smooth, thin object your tactile sense has taken in the information. When you realize that the object is a pen you are at the level of perception. Attentional deployment lies somewhere between sensation and perception, since registration and perception of a sensory event require attention.

The next level of information processing involves *coordinating mechanisms*. These are necessary because our senses take in information simultaneously, even though we may not be aware of this. For example, when you watch television you need to relate what you see on the screen to what you hear. Moreover, even though you are probably not aware of it at the time, your proprioceptive sense is undoubtedly working hard to maintain your postural position.

The information processing system

Level four contains the all-important *interpretation mechanisms*. These allow you to understand and make sense of incoming information. Past experience helps here. Hence, when you hear a high-pitched continuous sound, your past experience with this type of sound tells you that it's some type of siren. It should be obvious that one's *interpretation* of information is intimately related to one's *response*. For example, hearing a siren while driving a car would cause one to pull over to the side of the road.

Level five contains the *memory systems*. Without these, everything really would go in one ear and out the other! Of course, it is far more complex than this. There are many "decisions"

Table 5

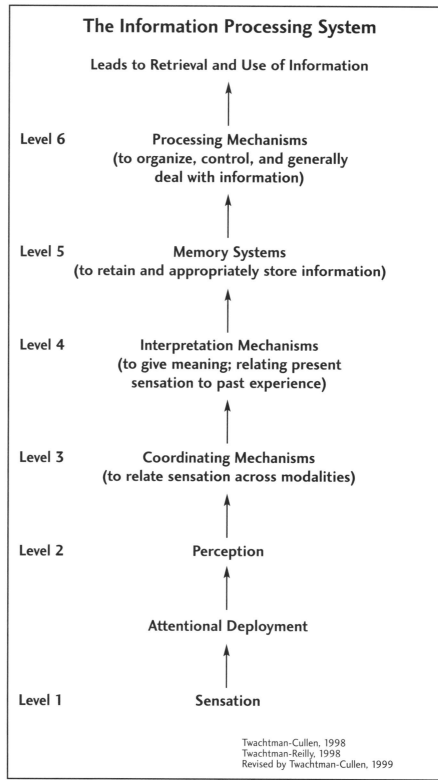

The Information Processing System

Leads to Retrieval and Use of Information

Level 6   **Processing Mechanisms**
(to organize, control, and generally deal with information)

Level 5   **Memory Systems**
(to retain and appropriately store information)

Level 4   **Interpretation Mechanisms**
(to give meaning; relating present sensation to past experience)

Level 3   **Coordinating Mechanisms**
(to relate sensation across modalities)

Level 2   **Perception**

                           Attentional Deployment

Level 1   **Sensation**

Twachtman-Cullen, 1998
Twachtman-Reilly, 1998
Revised by Twachtman-Cullen, 1999

to make, though most of these are automatic and hence below the level of our awareness. For example, decisions must be made regarding whether a particular piece of information is more appropriately stored in *short term memory,* where it will be available for relatively immediate use; or, whether it should be sent to the *long term memory* unit, where it can be available on a long term basis; or even whether it should be retained at all. It should be obvious that the decisions at this level of processing have implications vis-à-vis the availability of information for retrieval and use. Hence, *if information is not retained in memory, it won't be available for later retrieval and use.* Likewise, if it is *inappropriately stored* in memory, *retrieval and use will be compromised,* as well.

Level six, the final level of information processing actually houses the processing mechanisms themselves—that is, those processes that organize, control, and otherwise handle the flow of information so that it can be retrieved efficiently and used effectively. These mechanisms are known as the *executive functions,* and serve to oversee information processing. They will be discussed more fully in the next section of this chapter.

The link between information storage and retrieval

Before moving on, the following analogy may be helpful in understanding the implications of information processing deficits. Consider a very cluttered and disorganized closet into which everything is stuffed and in disarray. You're late for work, but you need to find the mate to the shoe you are wearing. You open the closet door and begin to indiscriminately pull things out, making an even bigger mess of things. How easy do you think it will be to find what you are looking for under these circumstances—being in a hurry, and dealing with the disorganization? Consider now the same task (that of finding a shoe), but a very different closet, one that contains a modular system for organization. In this closet there is a place for everything, and everything is in its place. Do you think it will be easier (and less anxiety provoking) to find what you are looking for? Moral of story: The brains of neurotypical people store information in an organized and eminently retrievable fashion, much like the modular closet in the example above. The brains of students with ASD may be thought of as storing information in a heap (i.e., in a disorganized and haphazard manner). As a result, *their processing of information tends to be slow and/or deficient, making retrieval and use of information an extremely cumbersome and time-consuming procedure.* Further, *stress and anxiety operate to make information processing even more difficult!* Please remember this when your students have difficulty answering questions (retrieving information) in the heat of the cognitively demanding moment in the classroom. Above all, don't make matters worse by urging them to hurry or insisting on a full sentence!

An interdependent system

Individual variations aside, it is still fair to say that *all* students with autism spectrum disorders experience information processing difficulty at some level, to one degree or another, and that processing glitches may occur *anywhere* in the system. Moreover, because of the *interdependence* among the various components in the information processing system, *abnormalities in one area can and do negatively impact functioning in another.* Consider again the concept of abnormal response to sensation. It is easy to see that abnormal input at Level one will produce abnormal output at Level six. For example, if a nearsighted individual perceives the *F* on an eye chart to be a *P*, his/her verbal output will reflect this abnormal input (i.e., s/he will call out the letter *P*).

Finally, the ability to efficiently and effectively process information so that it can be retrieved and used when needed has a lot to do with the integrity of the executive control mechanisms that oversee this complex, multidimensional activity. Unfortunately, as will be seen in the next section of this chapter, problems are found here, as well.

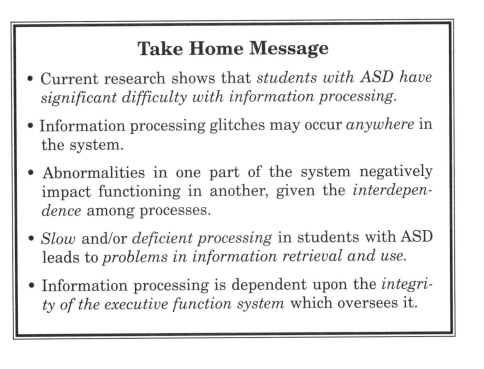

Take Home Message

- Current research shows that *students with ASD have significant difficulty with information processing.*

- Information processing glitches may occur *anywhere* in the system.

- Abnormalities in one part of the system negatively impact functioning in another, given the *interdependence* among processes.

- *Slow* and/or *deficient processing* in students with ASD leads to *problems in information retrieval and use.*

- Information processing is dependent upon the *integrity of the executive function system* which oversees it.

Executive Function: The "High Priestess" of the Cognitive System

Reducing the definition of *executive function (EF)* to its simplest level, it is the ability to do all that it takes to keep your mind on what you are doing in order to accomplish a given task. Though the definition is a simple one to understand, it is far more encompassing than it appears at first glance. The key phrase is *to do all that it takes,* and indeed, it takes a great deal! Let's examine what it takes to keep one's mind on what one is doing. For one thing, it takes the ability to *maintain attention*; that is, to concentrate on the job at hand. In order to do this, we must *control our impulses* (e.g., the desire to leave the task and do something else when we get bored, or when the going gets rough). Likewise, we need to *keep ourselves free from distractions* which interfere with attention. We also need to be able to *engage in mental planning and problem solving*. Both of these activities require *flexibility*, so that if Plan A doesn't work out, we can move to Plan B, and if that doesn't work out we can make the adjustments necessary in order to meet with success. We also need to be flexible enough to *transition* to a new situation or activity—or even a new way of looking at something— when necessary. Properly working executive function mechanisms also enable us not

Components of the executive function system

only to *apply* skills, but also to *self-monitor* our behavior, so that we can make the required adjustments to accommodate the situation. Finally, intact executive function mechanisms enable us to *keep our plans and goals uppermost in our minds* so that we can keep ourselves on track.

Most of us perform these executive function tasks quite effortlessly, though it is important to note that, as was the case with theory of mind, executive function activities too, are situation dependent. For example, *interest in the task helps to maintain attention, and stave off distractions*. This is true for all people, and a useful piece of information to keep in mind when dealing with students with ASD. Conversely, *lack of interest or desire leaves one more vulnerable to distractions and impulsive behavior*. For example, housework can be a pleasant diversion when it prevents one from having to prepare a difficult-to-write report!

 Neurotypical diversity

While most of us have enough executive function ability to perform life's daily tasks adequately, there is nonetheless a great deal of variability among neurotypical people in EF ability. On the one hand there are those EF "geniuses" that are highly organized and thus able to accomplish well, in a short time, tasks that others find difficult and cumbersome. And then there are those whom we call, "Jacks of all trades, masters of none," to characterize their inability to keep their eyes on the goal, as well as their propensity to flit from thing to thing. It must be emphasized, however, that both types of individuals—though widely disparate in their executive function ability—are nevertheless within the normal range of EF functioning.

 Manifestations of executive function deficit in ASD

Students with ASD evidence marked difficulty with several aspects of executive function. Unlike neurotypical people, students with ASD are prone to *distractibility* and *impulsivity*. They are known to be *rigid* and *inflexible* in both their thoughts and actions. Hence, when something goes wrong, instead of making adjustments, they might instead have a tantrum or engage in aggressive or self-injurious behavior. *Transition difficulty is a well-recognized autistic trait*, reflecting the students' lack of future orientation and their tendency to get stuck in the present. Finally, although they often go unrecognized, *difficulties in applying behavioral strategies and self-monitoring are stable, albeit insidious characteristics*

of these students. An example may help to clarify this issue. Students with ASD often demonstrate ability in one situation, but not in another. When paras and other caregivers observe that the child is capable of a particular desirable behavior, and in fact exhibits it in certain situations (e.g., in the therapy room when prompted), they often make an understandable but unfortunate assumption—that the student has mastered the behavior, and hence is ready to "take it on the road." Thus, when the student fails to engage in the behavior in other situations and places where it is called for, s/he is judged to be noncompliant (i.e., *unwilling* to perform). *The problem here, however, is not one of noncompliance, but rather one in which executive function impairment plays a major role.* Among the many other factors which could be operating (e.g., problems with comprehension or generalization, failing to recognize the need for the behavior in a new situation, etc.), there is most likely also a failure in the executive function mechanisms of *application* and *self-monitoring.* Furthermore, the well-known generalization difficulty evidenced by individuals with ASD may reflect, at least in part, their deficits in executive function. *Bottom Line:* Don't *assume* that because a behavior is exhibited in a relatively simple and *supported* environment, that the student is capable of executing and self-monitoring that same behavior in a more complex and less protected "real world" environment. In fact, it is best to *avoid assumptions* altogether!

💡 Bottom line

The Cumulative Effects of Executive Function Deficits

When each of the discrete elements of executive function deficit is taken together, the overall effect on the individual is such as to create *significant and pervasive problems in planning and organization.* For example, these students have difficulty holding information "on line," *particularly if it is rendered orally.* Thus, they have trouble following directions, keeping track of things, remembering what to do, and following tasks through to completion. They tend to forget to bring important books and papers home, or to the next class. They are often late, seeming always to be playing "catch-up ball," but never quite catching up! Very young students may react tearfully or aggressively to transitions, while older students

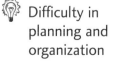

💡 Difficulty in planning and organization

manifest their transition difficulties in more subtle ways; that is, by a *lack of readiness* and *general disorganization*. Long term assignments such as term papers and reports are very difficult for these students to manage, since they have trouble with advanced planning and parceling out segments of time, both of which are involved in such assignments. Likewise, homework tends to be a nightmare for students with ASD (and for their parents, as well!). There are several factors that may be operating here. Students with EF deficits often spend inordinate amounts of time on one small aspect of the homework assignment, quite literally running out of time for the others. Further, their distractibility impedes sustained concentration, and their impulsivity often causes them to pursue other more appealing pursuits when they should be completing assignments. Sadly, even though their parents wage nightly battles in the "homework wars," the valiant and laborious efforts of these loyal "warriors" are no match for the executive function deficits fueling those wars.

The executive function–behavioral connection

As if these significant and pervasive problems are not devastating enough, the most common reaction to the above-noted set of behaviors is to judge the student as lazy, noncompliant, and willful. *Such judgments have the effect of punishing students with ASD for their disability.* This most likely occurs because when the behaviors described above are seen in *neurotypical* students—*those without executive function deficits*—they may well stem from some degree of laziness or noncompliance. Paras and other caregivers are cautioned *not* to apply standards that may be appropriate for neurotypical children to students with EF dysfunction, based upon the following: Students with autism spectrum disorders have *special* needs (EF deficits), that require *special* understanding (not summary judgments), and most importantly, *special* supports and accommodations that address their planning and organizational needs.

Take Home Message

- Executive function deficits in ASD can cause the following discrete symptoms: *distractibility; impulsivity; inflexibility/rigidity; and transition difficulty.*

- Discrete deficits, in turn, create problems in higher-order activities such as *problem solving and mental planning; organizational skills, self-monitoring, and application of skills.*

- *Interest in a task or activity helps to maintain attention* and stave off distractions.

- Don't assume that because a behavior is exhibited in a relatively simple and *supported* environment, that the student is capable of *executing* or *self-monitoring* that same behavior in a more complex and less protected "real world" environment.

- Likewise, don't assume that the student *understands* the need for the behavior in the natural situation.

- *The student's significant and pervasive problems in planning and organization should never be mistaken for laziness or noncompliance.*

- Students with ASD require *special understanding* and *special supports* that address their planning and organizational needs.

Chapter Seven

Getting to Know Your Student
High Functioning Autism or Asperger Syndrome: Does it Really Matter?

The series of descriptions which follows contains important information regarding the similarities and differences between *high functioning autism* and *Asperger syndrome* from my perspective. In order to enable you to more fully appreciate the origin of this material, and what I intend in presenting it, a bit of background information is in order.

I became involved in the clinical aspects of Asperger syndrome approximately two years *before* it became an official diagnosis in *DSM-IV*. Notwithstanding its lack of inclusion in earlier manuals, Asperger syndrome had nonetheless been a well-recognized syndrome in Europe for many years, having been described initially by Hans Asperger, an Austrian psychiatrist, in 1944. Although Asperger's paper was written only one year after Leo Kanner described a group of similar children in the United States, knowledge of the syndrome bearing his name was virtually unknown in this country until mid 1990.

In January, 1992, prior to the publication of *DSM-IV,* I was asked to provide consultation services for a 4-year-old boy who had recently been diagnosed with Asperger syndrome. His father, a major television news anchor in my State, decided to do a two-part news special on this "new" disorder. As the family's consultant, I appeared on the program to discuss educational issues. The response to the program from the audience was overwhelmingly positive, causing the TV station to advertise that it would re-broadcast the program one week later. Many viewers, recognizing similarities between the little boy on TV and the children of their friends and relatives in other parts of the country, stood poised by their VCR's so that they could videotape the program and send the tapes far and wide. Referrals began to pour into my office, and like all of you, I learned while in the trenches. Such was my "baptism by fire" initiation into what I have termed the *topsy turvy world of Asperger syndrome*—a designation that underscores the erratic and volatile nature of the plight of these individuals as the least understood members on the autism spectrum continuum. The information contained within this chapter represents a compendium of what I have learned from the children, adolescents, and adults with Asperger syndrome who have been my teachers over these many years.

First, the "disclaimers." This comparison is based upon my personal clinical experience. While this experience is extensive, it is nonetheless *my experience*, and hence the information which follows is my *subjective* analysis of the differences—subtle at times—between the two diagnostic categories. I neither intend this comparison to serve as an exhaustive list of all of the possible symptoms found in these disorders, nor as the final word on the subject. What I do intend is to provide you with useful information regarding differences in how specific symptoms might "play out" in HFA and AS.

As you read along, you are urged to keep the following points in mind:

- The compendium which follows addresses *general tendencies*, as opposed to "hard core" absolutes; hence, there is overlap and "crossover" at times between categories.

- There are *exceptions to every rule* (but of course they help to "prove" the rule!).

- Not all things apply to all students, so read the little words like *often* and *may* because they convey important qualifying information.

- Pay attention to the *italics*, for they highlight important information and put the "spin" I intend on the material.

Before proceeding, it is important to note that the opinions expressed here are more applicable to students in later elementary, middle, and high school, as the boundaries between high functioning autism and Asperger syndrome are much more difficult to discern in very young children. To wit, I have seen a significant number of children who were initially diagnosed with autism, only to have that diagnosis changed (further refined?) to Asperger syndrome as they developed symptomatology more consistent with the latter. Dr. Lorna Wing, an internationally renowned expert in autism spectrum disorders has reported on this same phenomenon. The reasons for this are quite simple. Unlike diabetes and other disorders that are definitively diagnosed via blood tests, HFA and AS are *behaviorally defined syndromes*. As such, diagnosis will vary according to the knowledge base and analytical prowess of the diagnostician. It will also vary with respect to how the constellation of symptoms plays out in each individual child over time. For these reasons, diagnosis of autism spectrum disorders is more of an art than a science.

Blurred boundaries

Finally, please note that for the purposes of this comparison, I chose *only* those symptoms for which I regularly found *distinctive* differences between the two diagnostic categories. Less "robust" or obvious differences between the two disorders—though informative—are not included here.

Preference for Sameness

In high functioning autism there is a preference for sameness which often results in students' resistance to change in general, and new activities, people, and circumstances in particular. Though the preference is a strong and stable one, the behavior which these students exhibit does not seem particularly *driven*.

The preference for sameness one sees in autism may be construed as *elevated to an "art form" in Asperger syndrome*; that is, it takes on a *driven* quality, where thoughts and actions directed toward narrow and circumscribed interests appear obsessive and compulsive, rather than merely preferential. Although obsessive-compulsive disorder (OCD) can exist along with Asperger syndrome, use of the terms *obsessive/compulsive* here is more generic; that is, intended to underscore the students' *intense* desire to focus on only that which absorbs their interests—a desire to which they readily give in, rather than resist.

Attention

Students with HFA manifest problems in rapidly and flexibly shifting from one thing to another and/or in over-focusing (i.e., getting stuck) on some things to the detriment of others. They do not seem *as vulnerable* to environmental distractions as students with Asperger syndrome, since their absorption (i.e., over-focusing) seems to "gate" the effect of external distractions (i.e., keeps them at bay*)*.

In Asperger syndrome, the attentional difficulties strongly resemble those that are seen is ADD or ADHD. Thus, students with AS tend to be more drawn to distractions and more obviously *impulsive* than those with autism, per se. In fact, it is this specific quality of attentional difficulty that causes many diagnosticians to incorrectly diagnose many AS students as manifesting *only* ADD or ADHD.

Response to Stimulation

High stimulation often causes hyperarousal in students with HFA. This may cause their sensitive systems to become overloaded, and hence to "shut down."

The fine line between optimal and "over the edge"

In contrast, students with AS *appear to need more intense stimulation* than those with HFA, as they are often observed seeking it out. It may be that the well-known tendency of students with AS to "push the buttons" of their caregivers reflects their desire (need?) for heightened stimulation. A word of caution, however, is in order. *There is an extremely narrow band between optimal stimulation and over stimulation in students with Asperger syndrome which makes regulation of stimulation very difficult.* Moreover, once "over the edge," students with Asperger syndrome are as adversely affected by high stimulation as are those with autism.

Response to Stimulant Medication

Stimulant medication often (but not always) *worsens* symptoms in students with HFA, causing irritability, discomfort, and hyperarousal.

Stimulant medication often (but not always) *improves* the distractibility and impulsivity which negatively impacts students' ability to selectively attend and concentrate. *There are some instances, however, where the side effects associated with stimulant medication far outweigh the positive effects which such medication may have on attention.*

Note: The decision regarding whether or not to use medication rests with the physician; however, *when medications are used their effects on students need to be monitored on a continuous basis over time.*

Exercise vigilance regarding the effects of medication

Differences in Imagination

Students with HFA may demonstrate the rudiments of imagination in some situations, particularly where there has been prior training and opportunities for repetition and practice. Even so, *imagination will be underdeveloped and markedly impoverished*, even when compared to children with other developmental disabilities.

Students with AS exhibit more *varied* responses with respect to imagination than do students with HFA. At times they may demonstrate an *over-developed*, or *aberrant* use of imagination in which the boundary between reality and fantasy is blurred. For example, if these children see "special effect" stunts on television or in movies they may try to reproduce them, completely unmindful that their actions may be dangerous to themselves or others. Sometimes the play behavior of students with Asperger syndrome looks very sophisticated, when in reality it is scripted almost verbatim from a favorite video or television program. *Despite superficial sophistication, there is nonetheless a nonreciprocal, controlling aspect to the play behavior of children with Asperger syndrome* which, though more impressive than that seen in HFA, still stands in marked contrast to the play behavior of neurotypical peers.

 A word of caution

Note: Because of difficulties which many children with AS have in distinguishing reality from fantasy, *it is important for caregivers to monitor what these children see or read, since their lack of social understanding, common sense, and judgment may be inimical both to their well-being and that of others.*

Social Behavior

There is an apparent lack of preference for, or interest in, social interaction in students with HFA. When interactions do occur, they tend to be at the initiation of others, and to center around factual, reality-based material. Moreover, students with high functioning autism tend to evidence greater passivity in social situations than do those with Asperger syndrome.

Students with AS, in sharp contrast to those with HFA, may appear quite "social," particularly when engaged in topics of intense personal interest. In such situations they may strive to *impose* their interests onto others *without regard to social distress signals* in their "partners." Though active and social seeking in such circumstances, their social behavior is nonetheless atypical for its *excessive, unilateral*, and *nonreciprocating* quality. Further, in contrast to students with HFA, those with AS appear to have a greater awareness of their social difficulties, particularly as they approach adolescence. For example, many students with AS express not only their *desire for friends,* but also their *despondence* over not having them. Even when this is the case, however, these students *lack the socially skilled behavior required to establish and maintain friendships.* Hence, they may say or do things that are off-putting to other children. In a very real sense, they are "their own worst enemies" in social situations, not from a willful or intentional perspective, but rather from the perspective of their social disability.

Communication and Language

There is generally a *less sophisticated use of language* both in terms of vocabulary and verbal expression in HFA than what is seen in students with AS. There is also greater passivity and less spontaneity, as well. Overall pragmatic communication ability, though considerably better than what is seen in students at the lower end of the autism spectrum continuum, is nevertheless not up to the level of those with Asperger syndrome.

There is *greater sophistication,* and often a *pedantic, professorial quality,* in all aspects of communication and language behavior in Asperger syndrome, than what is seen in HFA. This sophistication is more apparent when these students express factual information. *Superficially,* language appears either normal (as in the case of grammar and syntax), or advanced (as in the case of vocabulary development). *Students with Asperger syndrome speak more metaphorically (i.e., in round-about, idiosyncratic ways)* than those with HFA, particularly when trying to express complex feelings and emotions—areas of notorious difficulty for them. Simply stated, language use in Asperger syndrome, unlike that in high functioning autism, is characterized by the unscientific (but eminently descriptive) word *pizzazz!*

Note: The *superficially* sophisticated use of language in Asperger syndrome is quite misleading, causing caregivers to be blinded by these students' strengths, at the same time they are unmindful of their weaknesses in areas which support communication and language, but which are far less obvious (e.g., comprehension, information processing, executive functioning, etc.).

Look beneath the surface of superficially impressive language

Response to Sensation

The sensory issues in HFA may be thought of as "middle of the road"—more *obvious* than those seen in Asperger syndrome, but having less of an impact on functioning than occurs in more classic autism.

The sensory issues in Asperger syndrome are not only more *subtle,* but also more *deceptive.* Sometimes they may present as aggression when a youngster, put off by light touch, pushes someone away. At other times they may present as clumsiness or awkwardness, when proprioceptive feedback is deficient.

Diagnostic Issues

Diagnosis of autism is usually early and more straightforward than it is in Asperger syndrome. That said, *differential diagnosis* to determine whether the child has HFA or AS is more difficult, particularly in very young children since, as noted earlier in this chapter, the boundaries between the two diagnostic categories blur at younger age levels.

Diagnostic issues in Asperger syndrome are markedly complex, given the relative subtleties in symptomatology, the similarity to HFA, and the confusion inherent in *DSM-IV*. Consequently, *misdiagnosis* of children with Asperger syndrome is quite common, particularly since some of their discrete symptoms resemble those associated with other disorders. While much could be said, suffice it to say, that *the issue of diagnosis in Asperger syndrome is at best thorny, and at worst nightmarish,* as the following summary suggests:

- When a diagnosis of Asperger syndrome is made it usually comes *later* than is the case in HFA.

- It is not uncommon for the child to be diagnosed with a variety of different labels, *before* Asperger syndrome is recognized.

- It is quite common for individuals with AS to go *undiagnosed* for years.

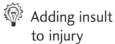 Adding insult to injury

Note: The most "charged" *misdiagnosis* of Asperger Syndrome, in my opinion, is that of *Oppositional Defiant Disorder*, as this label ignores the neurological symptoms and problems with sensation that accompany Asperger syndrome, and confers "blame" on the child. I strongly feel that students with AS are not only *not* well served by this label, but also that *such a label is actually inimical to their best interests,* since it *misrepresents* their disability.

Behavioral Judgments

There is *less* of a tendency in HFA to label students as willful or volitional, even when behavior is considered inappropriate. In other words, their behavior seems more *reactive* than deliberate or calculated.

Students with Asperger syndrome present with a more complex behavioral picture. Some students with AS are quite oppositional, to a point that defies logic. For example, one parent described this oppositionality in the following manner: *"John disagrees with everything I say. If I say the sky is blue, he says no it's white. If I tell him to use a soup spoon for his soup, he refuses and picks up a teaspoon."* In order to understand the motivation behind this behavior it is necessary to look beneath the surface. In many of the students I've seen, oppositionality serves as a subterfuge for the individual's desperate desire for control. In other students, it represents the manifestation of a faulty rule system. For example, if the student has experienced significant discomfort when s/he has been cooperative and agreeable, s/he might associate the discomfort with acquiescence, and hence come to the erroneous conclusion (i.e., rule) that oppositionality is the way to avoid discomfort. Regardless of the internal motivation for such behavior, it is easy to understand why these students are frequently labeled *willful, volitional,* and *obstinate.* The subtlety of their symptoms and their greater sophistication in language probably contribute to the propensity to "blame" them for behavioral excesses, on the theory that they "should know better." Moreover, their desire for stimulation undoubtedly looks as though they are deliberately trying to provoke people.

Note: The following explanation may help you to take the perspective of the student with AS before making a judgment of willfulness: When students with Asperger syndrome "push the buttons" of their caregivers, they do so *not* for the *psychological* (i.e., upsetting) effect it has on the caregivers, but rather for the *physical* (i.e., stimulating) effect which *caregiver reaction* has on *them.* This is not to say that students with AS are never willful, but rather to implore you to *take the perspective of the student* so that you may consider each individual situation on its own merits.

Beware of shortsighted judgments

Summary

Overall, the preceding comparison illustrates that while high functioning autism and Asperger syndrome share many of the same symptoms, *it is the particular way in which these symp-*

Qualitatively different vs. categorically different

toms play out that constitutes the essence of the difference between the two disorders. In my opinion, these differences are mostly *qualitative;* that is, one of degree and/or manner of presentation, as opposed to one in which each disorder contains *categorically different* symptoms. To summarize, the constellation of symptoms in high functioning autism plays out in such a way that the deficits are more apparent and hence, clearly *recognizable* as autistic disorder. In other words, *the road from classic autism to HFA is straighter and more easily traveled for this particular spectrum disorder.*

 Blinded by their strengths

Asperger syndrome, on the other hand, often defies recognition. Not only are its deficits less obvious, but their manner of presentation is also more deceptive. At times these students appear too social or too sophisticated language-wise to have a disorder along the autism spectrum continuum. These factors, along with their apparent willfulness, not only cause diagnosticians to become blinded by the strengths of these children, but also lead them to look elsewhere for diagnostic labels that appear to better "fit" the symptom picture. Hence, *the road from high functioning autism to Asperger syndrome has more twists and turns in it and makes for a bumpier ride* than does its counterpart in HFA. Perhaps the best characterization of the differences between the two disorders is the one offered by a parent of two children—one with high-functioning autism, and one with Asperger syndrome. In his "expert" opinion, *"Asperger syndrome is autism with an attitude!"*

 Different expressions of the same basic disorder

All things considered, the safest and best rule of thumb at this point in time is to consider high functioning autism and Asperger syndrome to be *different expressions of the same basic disorder.* The answer to the question posed in the title of this chapter, *"Does it really matter whether an individual receives a diagnosis of high functioning autism or Asperger syndrome?"* is a little tricky. On the one hand, students with AS require the *same* types of supports, services, and teaching experiences that those with HFA require. On the other hand, however, the oft-seen oppositionality and willful, volitional *appearance* of students with Asperger syndrome, leaves them vulnerable to misunderstanding and erroneous judgments. Hence, in my opinion, it is important to acknowledge the ways in which their deficits both resemble, and yet differ from those of their better understood counterparts on the autism spectrum continuum. It is hoped that knowledge of the qualitative differences between students with AS and HFA may help not only to counteract faulty impressions, but also to bring about a greater appreciation of the topsy turvy world in which the student with Asperger syndrome resides.

Take Home Message

- Autism and Asperger syndrome are considered *different expressions of the same basic disorder.*

- While high functioning autism and Asperger syndrome *share many similarities*, there are also *important differences* in the presentation of symptoms.

- Students with Asperger syndrome "inhabit" a topsy turvy world, given that the willful and volitional *appearance* of their behavior leads to *misunderstanding* of their motivations.

- Despite *qualitative* differences in the presentation of symptoms, students with high functioning autism and Asperger syndrome share *similar educational needs*.

PART TWO

The "Art and Science"
of Being a Para *Pro*

Chapter Eight

General Overview of Paraprofessional Support
A New Breed for a New Century

Since their emergence on the educational scene in the mid twentieth century, paraprofessional support personnel have grown in numbers, duties, responsibilities, and stature. For the most part, paras of an earlier time functioned primarily as *non-instructional* personnel, assisting teachers with such things as bulletin boards, clerical tasks, and hallway/recess duties. While these tasks are a necessary and important aspect of school life, they do not *directly* affect student learning.

As schools changed, so did the role of paraprofessionals. And nothing brought about more significant change both for schools and paras than the commitment to educating students with disabilities in public school settings. This created a need for a whole new breed of paras—one in which paraprofessionals moved from noninstructional duties as their *primary* responsibility, to direct instructional student support. With this they took on more specialized and comprehensive duties, moving from a primarily adjunctive position, to one that was *integral* to the educational care of students with special needs.

Notwithstanding that paraprofessionals have been called upon to perform an increasing number of duties which require a more sophisticated level of skill development, training opportunities *specifically designed for paras* are virtually nonexistent. Indeed, there seems to be a lack of recognition that paraprofessionals may need a *different type of in-service education plan* than that of teachers. Hence, when training

The unsuitability of the "one size fits all" training model

opportunities do exist, they typically follow a generic, "one size fits all" model. Moreover, it is still a relative rarity for school districts (except perhaps the most enlightened!) to grant paras release time to attend general training seminars outside of school which address the specific disabilities manifested by their students. Many paraprofessionals who attend these sessions do so at their own expense—a tribute to their dedication and desire to meet their students' educational needs.

In the next few pages I will address paraprofessional support from both a general and generic frame of reference, leaving the discussion of *specific* duties and responsibilities for the next chapter. This information is intended for *all* paraprofessionals who have *direct instructional responsibilities for students with special needs*—particularly those with *significant cognitive issues*—regardless of program philosophy or educational setting (i.e., inclusive classroom, resource room, or segregated facility). This manual takes no philosophical position whatsoever with respect to these issues, since they are not felt to be germane to the topics addressed in this manual.

A "Work-in-Progress"

The first thing that must be said about your role as a one-to-one instructional support person is that your role is still evolving. As such you are a "work-in-progress!" To make your job even more challenging, you are required to serve two masters—student and teacher. Thus, in a very real sense your role is one of *preeminent support*, a term which superficially appears to be an oxymoron, but which on closer scrutiny clearly captures the precise nature of your job. In other words, while you have a "front and center," *preeminent* role in the educational life of your student, it is a role that is nonetheless *supportive* (to both teacher and student) in its execution. To do this well requires that you keep both the *preeminent* and *supportive* aspects of your role in balance, a task that is more easily said than done. This crucial point will be further elaborated at the end of this chapter.

 The division of labor

First, let's examine the implications of your *dual responsibility* to both the teacher you assist and the student you serve. For one thing, you are an integral member of your student's instructional team. That said, it is not easy to be a team player unless you know what your position on the team is. (I doubt that Yogi Berra would have done a very good job for the New York Yankees if, instead of maintaining his position as catcher, he merely wandered aimlessly around the field trying to catch the ball!). Generally speaking, *you are not on the team to develop instructional plans*. That responsibility falls to the teacher. You do, however, have the important job of *implementing* those plans, but only *under the direction and supervision of the teacher*. Likewise, certified staff have the responsibility for assessing overall student progress and for educational decision making. For the most part, the parceling out of these general responsibilities is outside of our control—laid down as it were by State and Federal education laws. This division of responsibilities makes perfect educational sense, for not only is the teacher *responsible,* but also *accountable* for the overall instructional program. Hence, when educational decisions or practices are questioned, it is the teacher who must "step up to the plate" and either defend them or accept responsibility for any problems that occur. *Bottom line*: If the buck stops with the teacher in terms of accountability, then s/he needs to assume responsibility for educational decision making. This is in no way intended to demean the important role of the paraprofessional, but rather to distinguish it from that of the teacher.

Bottom line

Perspectives on the Duties and Responsibilities of Paraprofessional Support

Your responsibility to the student you serve requires a blend of art and science. *Your first duty is to understand both some general information about the disability your student manifests, and the particular way in which the symptoms affect him or her.* If you are the para of a student with an autism spectrum disorder, the information contained within the first seven chapters of this manual should go a long way toward fulfilling the first part of this duty. Only careful *observation* of your particular student will fulfill the second part. If, however, you are the para of a student with a disability other than ASD, I recommend that you use the informational structure of the first seven chapters as a guideline for obtaining the kind of information you need to better understand your student. For example, try to obtain information regarding your

The importance of understanding both the student and the disability

student's ability to comprehend, process, and express information, as well as that related to *organizational skills* (i.e., *executive function ability*) and *perspective taking* (i.e., *theory of mind*). Students with cognitive disabilities other than ASD often evidence problems in these important areas of functioning. For example, the greatest area of overlap between Asperger syndrome and Attention Deficit Disorder, with or without hyperactivity, is in the area of executive function deficit. Moreover, current thought on the subject of ADD/ADHD suggests the presence of perspective taking problems and subtle difficulty in the area of social skills development. As such, much of the information on these subjects within this manual is directly applicable to students with ADD and ADHD. The form entitled, *Getting to Know Your Student with Special Needs,* located at the end of this chapter represents a *generic prototype* for obtaining the type of information you need for any student, regardless of disability category.

Your second duty is to obtain some general information about your student's learning style, preferences, and needs so that tasks and activities can be presented in a manner that facilitates learning. For example, if careful observation reveals that your particular student learns best visually (as is usually the case in ASD), then a heavy reliance on auditory input would be inimical to his or her best learning interests. The *Learning Style Protocol* located at the end of this chapter contains information which can help you determine your student's preferences and needs regarding both learning and instructional style, as well as those related to instructional design and reinforcement. This protocol can be used for students with a variety of disabilities, and is one that paras and teachers can and should complete *jointly*.

 Obtain information on learning style, preferences, and needs

 Maintain confidentiality

Another very important duty you have is to, first and foremost, *maintain confidentiality*. This is not simply a matter of *not* using names, but rather of *maintaining silence*. Many a confidence has been breached (albeit inadvertently), when specific details have sufficed to reveal a student's identity. Confidentiality should also extend to others in the school community. As a para you will no doubt be privy to information that affects the privacy of other students in the classroom. Hence, your position requires your ongoing commitment to the maintenance of confidentiality with respect to *all* students and the school community as a whole, not just to the student to whom you have been assigned.

Further, if you are to perform the important job you have to do to the best of your ability, *you need to know the expectations of the teacher with whom you work*. In a perfect world, the teacher would clearly delineate them so that you would know exactly where your responsibilities begin and end. As we all know, this is not a perfect world, so some of the responsibility for obtaining this information will necessarily fall to you. Consequently, *don't settle for discovering the teacher's expectations bit by bit as the days evolve*, a practice that will not only keep you off-balance, but will also adversely affect your work with your student, and your relationship with the teacher. Don't make assumptions either. Instead, *be proactive!* Find out what the teacher expects of you by asking direct questions. After all, the *quality of your performance* is directly related to the *quality of the information* you receive regarding what is expected (and frankly, what is not!).

Seek out the expectations of the teacher

Relationship Considerations: Doing Your Part

Before moving on, it is important to consider the teacher - para relationship, since problems here will surely negatively impact both the student and the classroom culture, in general. As in all relationships, the basic ingredient for an excellent working relationship here is that of *mutual trust*. Breakdowns in trust occur for several reasons, but they usually have their roots in *too little information*, *too many assumptions*, and *poor communication*. Since trust is a two-way street, you don't have "eminent domain" over it. Notwithstanding, you can and should do your part. This brings us full circle—back to your role of providing *preeminent support,* and the need to *balance* both aspects of these seemingly contradictory responsibilities. If you err too much in the direction of *preeminence,* you usurp the role of the teacher. That does little to engender the teacher's trust, and an awful lot to create resentment. If, on the other hand, you err in the direction of taking too subordinate a role in the student's life—quite literally waiting to be told what to do in every situation—you put too much responsibility on the teacher. This causes him or her to view you as more of a liability than an asset! This, too,

The importance of balance in preeminent support

causes resentment, and a fair amount of frustration as well—hardly the stuff of which trust is made. To be sure, if trust is to be mutual the teacher must do his or her part as well; however, what someone else does is not within your control. What *you* choose to do, however, is within your control. Consequently, if you do your part you will go a long way toward fulfilling an important (albeit intangible) aspect of your job. Further, you will also set the stage for an excellent working relationship with not only the teacher, but indirectly with the student, as well, since s/he is the ultimate beneficiary of the teacher-para relationship.

 Being right vs. doing right

There is one additional thing that needs to be said about caregiver behavior that everyone recognizes, but nobody likes to acknowledge. This has to do with ego involvement. Stated simply, when caregivers (paras or teachers) become too vested in *being right,* rather than in *doing right* by their students, they allow their egos to inflate their sense of self-importance to the detriment of those in their care. The red flag for unhealthy ego involvement is *defensiveness.* Where you see it, expect also to see too much self-interest and not enough student interest! As a consultant I am painfully aware of the ravages of defensiveness. When caregivers are defensive they are close-minded and self-protective, interpreting constructive input directed toward student learning as criticism directed toward themselves. Not to belabor the point, I reiterate: *Where there is too much self-interest, there is too little student interest, and this is always detrimental to the student.* Hence, a final word (both literally and figuratively!) for *all* caregivers:

Take Home Message

- Your first responsibility is to *understand both the student and the disability s/he manifests.*

- It is vitally important that you obtain information about the student's learning style, needs, and preferences.

- The maintenance of confidentiality in *all* matters is a top priority.

- *Be proactive* with respect to seeking out information regarding what is expected (and what is not!).

- Do what is necessary to *establish and maintain a relationship of trust with the teacher.*

- Strive for *balance* in your role of *preeminent support.*

- *Check your ego at the school house door!*

Getting to Know Your Student with Special Needs

For maximal effectiveness, this form should be filled out jointly by teacher and para. Please circle all that apply, using your best judgment. Use narrative and examples to provide a rationale for your selections, where appropriate.

Student: Respondent: Date:

I. Communication and Language Behavior

A. What is your student's primary mode of communication?
Predominantly verbal (circle all that apply)
single words / sentences / narrative discourse

Minimally verbal (circle all that apply)
single words / 2–3 word phrases

Predominantly nonverbal (circle all that apply)
non specific sounds/gestures / manual signs / pictures / computerized system / combination system / aberrant behavior / lacks a reliable, conventional communication system

B. What is your student's level of comprehension?
understands almost everything even without benefit of context / understands only in context and within learned routines / significant impairment in comprehension

C. How well does your student follow verbal directions?
almost always / sometimes / rarely / never / requires visual cues and repetition

II. Social Understanding and Expression

A. How well does your student understand social behavior/situations?
responds appropriately / responds inappropriately

B. What is your student's level of social expression?
social seeking, appropriate / social seeking, aberrant / appears interested / appears disinterested / socially appropriate / socially inappropriate (describe)

III. Interests and Activities

A. How would you describe your student's interests?
variety of interests / few interests / narrow & circumscribed / unusual interests (specify)

B. How would you describe your student's level of participation?
readily participates in a wide variety of activities / needs prompts to participate / resists participation / appears to lack interest in activities / prefers solitary activities (specify)

IV. Sensory Issues Affecting Student Behavior

A. Which of the following areas appear to be problematic?
tactile / auditory / visual / olfactory / gustatory / vestibular / proprioceptive / NA

B. How do sensory issues affect student behavior?
sensory seeking / avoidant behavior / becomes easily overstimulated / understimulated / other (describe)

V. Theory of Mind / Perspective Taking, and Empathy

A. Does your student appear to understand that different people have different points of view?
accepts other people's opinions even when they differ from his/her own / resists other's opinions when they differ from his/her own / intolerant of points of view other than his/her own

B. Does your student exhibit empathic behavior?
often / sometimes / rarely / never / shows no response to other's misfortunes / behaves inappropriately in the face of other's misfortunes (e.g. laughs) / unable to "share" other's feelings

VI. Information Processing Ability

A. How does your student handle the flow of information?
processes simple information normally / difficulty with complex information / slow or delayed processing / becomes overwhelmed / tunes out

B. Which factors help to facilitate information processing?
quiet environments / fewer people / repetition / visual supports / demonstration & modeling / reduction in complexity of information / other (specify)

VII. Executive Function Ability

A. Which areas of executive function deficit are problematic for your student?
distractible / impulsive / inflexible / difficulty with transitions / difficulty with mental planning / problem solving difficulty / problems in self-monitoring / difficulty applying skills

B. How would you describe your student's organizational ability?
highly organized / moderate problems in organization / disorganized / difficulty parceling out assignments / difficulty meeting deadlines / forgetful / other (specify)

C. Which factors help to improve organizational ability?
interest in task / visual cues and supports / templates for sequencing steps / written reminders / checklists / other (specify)

VIII. Miscellaneous Areas of Functioning

A. Does your student have seizures?
yes / no / controlled / uncontrolled

B. Is your student on medication?
yes / no / type (specify)

C. Does your student have allergies?
yes (specify) / no

D. Is your student on a special diet?
yes (specify) / no

E. Does your student exhibit aberrant behavior? (Self-injurious behavior is included here)
often / sometimes / rarely / never
If present, describe behavior(s) and circumstances under which it occurs

F. Does your student engage in self-stimulatory behavior?
often / sometimes / rarely / never
If present, describe behavior(s) and circumstances under which it occurs

G. What other issues impact your student's ability to be successful in school?

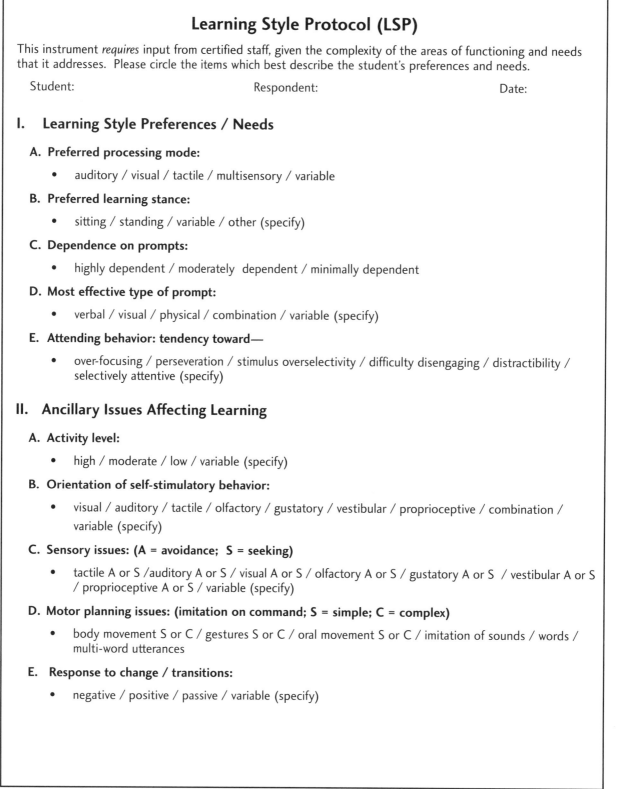

Learning Style Protocol (LSP)

This instrument *requires* input from certified staff, given the complexity of the areas of functioning and needs that it addresses. Please circle the items which best describe the student's preferences and needs.

Student: Respondent: Date:

I. Learning Style Preferences / Needs

A. Preferred processing mode:
- auditory / visual / tactile / multisensory / variable

B. Preferred learning stance:
- sitting / standing / variable / other (specify)

C. Dependence on prompts:
- highly dependent / moderately dependent / minimally dependent

D. Most effective type of prompt:
- verbal / visual / physical / combination / variable (specify)

E. Attending behavior: tendency toward—
- over-focusing / perseveration / stimulus overselectivity / difficulty disengaging / distractibility / selectively attentive (specify)

II. Ancillary Issues Affecting Learning

A. Activity level:
- high / moderate / low / variable (specify)

B. Orientation of self-stimulatory behavior:
- visual / auditory / tactile / olfactory / gustatory / vestibular / proprioceptive / combination / variable (specify)

C. Sensory issues: (A = avoidance; S = seeking)
- tactile A or S / auditory A or S / visual A or S / olfactory A or S / gustatory A or S / vestibular A or S / proprioceptive A or S / variable (specify)

D. Motor planning issues: (imitation on command; S = simple; C = complex)
- body movement S or C / gestures S or C / oral movement S or C / imitation of sounds / words / multi-word utterances

E. Response to change / transitions:
- negative / positive / passive / variable (specify)

III. Environmental / Instructional Style Preferences / Needs

A. Factors that facilitate attention:

- visual supports (specify) / repetition / "hands-on" / augmentation (specify) / structure / instruction in context / task familiarity / other (specify)

B. Factors that decrease attention:

- too few visual supports (too auditory) /excess noise / high-activity environments / high-demand environments / distractions (both visual & auditory) / other (specify)

IV. Instructional Design Preferences / Needs: How Does the Student Learn Best?

A. Preferred size of instructional unit:

- 1:1 / small group / large group / variable (specify)

B. Preferred mode of task presentation:

- explanation only / demonstration and modelling / explanation, demonstration, and modelling with visual cues as templates / multisensory / other (specify)

C. Task preferences:

- open-ended tasks / "close-ended" tasks / sedentary activities / tasks requiring movement / variable / other (specify)

D. Preferred supports:

- schedule / choice board / transition markers / turn markers / visual timers / organizational supports /other external supports (specify)

V. Reinforcement Preferences

A. Preferred mode of reinforcement:

- tangible (food) / privileges / free time / preferred activities or items / social / other (specify)

B. Preferred schedule of reinforcement:

- immediate / intermittent / variable (specify)

VI. Other Factors Influencing Learning Style (describe)

Chapter Nine

You're in the Trenches Now
The "Science" of Being a Para Pro

The big push for one-to-one paraprofessional support for students with special needs came in the mid 1980's, (not coincidentally) at about the same time the inclusive education movement began to pick up momentum. Those who argued that children with disabilities had a right to an education alongside their chronologically, age-appropriate typical peers, nonetheless couldn't argue convincingly against opponents' assertions that the pace of inclusive classrooms was too fast, and the regular educators too unprepared to deal with students with complex learning needs, particularly those with significant cognitive impairments. Enter the one-to-one para. Your job then was to assist the teacher so that s/he did not neglect the other students, and at the same time you were expected to facilitate the student's learning with respect to the classroom curriculum. An excellent idea on its face, but too shortsighted and simplistic to get the job done. After all, as you soon found out, you were ill-equipped to play Dorothy when there was no yellow brick road (in the way of training) leading you to Oz.

Within no time you found yourself mired in "corollary" issues (never mentioned in your job description, if indeed you even had one!). For students with significant cognitive impairments (depending upon age and functioning level) you were expected to deal with issues as diverse as toileting, aggression, self-injurious behavior, social-emotional development, tantrums, and/or self-stimulatory behavior, at the same time you were also expected to facilitate attention to subjects that, in many cases, your charges had little or no interest in learning. And most importantly, you were expected to either keep the student quiet, or remove him or her from the classroom so as not to disturb the chronologically, age-appropriate peers when your efforts failed. Thus, you hardly had time to get used to the trenches when you found yourselves immersed in the conflict of *how best to manage your student's best interests when they differed from those of his or her classmates.* This issue began to loom larger and larger, as students with disabilities—particularly those with autism and related conditions— learned eminently well the one lesson that paras and teachers never wanted to teach them: that *if they acted out, they got out* of situations that they found *unmeaningful, irrelevant,* and/or *aversive.* They learned that lesson so well, in fact, that it often derailed your efforts to facilitate their attention to task, and jeopardized their learning in the process. To make matters worse, your "training" was quite literally "on the job!" You had little advanced notice regarding the specifics of your assignment, for the simple reason that, in the beginning, nobody really knew exactly what your role as a one-to-one support person would (or should) be, particularly with respect to students with significant disabilities. The last fifteen years or so have provided a "track record" of one-to-one paraprofessional support, and as unenviable as that track record is in some respects, it nonetheless affords us the opportunity to learn from our mistakes, as well as from our successes.

 On the job "training"

Before proceeding, please read the following important "disclaimers" regarding the information in the next section of this manual:

- Although the term one-to-one is used throughout this manual it is acknowledged that in some settings the format for such support will be that of *small group (e.g., one para per two or three students).*

- *Don't be too literal!* Not all of the duties and responsibilities addressed apply to all students and situations.

- *Consider age and functioning level.* Only you can determine from the generic lists and information presented what is appropriate for your particular student.

- *Do not consider the duties and responsibilities covered in this section of the manual to be "finite."* There are an infinite number of things that could be done to facilitate the student's learning. Those presented here are only some of the more conventional ones.

- Use the ideas presented as *springboards* for your own creativity.

- *Read between the lines!* Try to get "a feel" for the rationale behind the duties and responsibilities that are outlined, particularly with respect to the detailed information on ASD given in the first several chapters, as it will help you to appreciate the need for *highly directive* support for students with autism spectrum disorders.

- *Read mindfully!* The information contained within these pages requires *mindful understanding*, rather than *mindless re-enactment*. The former has staying power and the capacity to ignite your own creativity. The latter has neither.

- *Keep your eye on the ball!* The goal is to be a para *pro*, not a robotic technician!

- *Use common sense* (and know that it is anything but *common!*).

Your number one responsibility as a direct instruction paraprofessional support person is to do just that—*render direct educational support to your student under the direction and supervision of the classroom teacher*. From time to time there will be ancillary duties, such as attending to the lunch count, or monitoring a reading group; however, these duties should not interfere with, nor overshadow your *primary responsibility—that of providing direct support to the student or students to whom you have been assigned*. If you feel that additional duties are preventing you from fulfilling this responsibility, it is critically important that you discuss your concerns with the classroom teacher so that accommodations may be made. After all, most likely your particular student has been assigned to you as a result of a Planning and Placement Team decision. To *not* fulfill your responsibilities to the student is to be in violation of the Individualized Education Plan (IEP). Hence, if you are not able to forge out an amicable arrangement with the teacher, it may be necessary for the principal to become involved to help facilitate one.

The para's primary responsibility

I have divided the duties and responsibilities of paraprofessional support staff into five categories for ease of handling only. Please be aware that *overlap* among categories does exist, and that the order of presentation within categories is strictly *arbitrary*, as opposed to hierarchical.

Peripheral Support

This category of support contains those essential duties and activities that have widespread, general applicability to students with special needs. They may be considered the "environmental staples" that enable students with cognitive impairment to better understand expectations and to generally feel more at ease in the classroom. Peripheral supports include visual schedules, choice/selection boards, visual timers, transition markers, and the like. This category of support also includes duties and responsibilities that are more supplemental to the curriculum, rather than rendered in direct implementation of it. Despite their more general and supplemental nature, *activities listed under this designation are no less important than those listed under other categories.* Table 6 lists the duties and responsibilities that come under this heading. Only those that require additional explanation will be discussed in greater detail here.

 Executive function props

Taking notes for students, highlighting important information, constructing visual supports (i.e., schedules, choice boards, etc.), and providing organizational aids may be considered *executive function props*, as they address the deficits related to executive dysfunction. Students with cognitive impairment, particularly those with ADD or ADHD, require these supports in order to function more effectively. Students with autism spectrum disorders need a *heavy dose* of EF supports. Their information processing difficulties, auditory weaknesses, and fine motor coordination problems combine to make it difficult for even the most able students with ASD to take down information in a timely and orderly fashion. In addition, their problems in the areas of social understanding, inferential reasoning, and theory of mind make it difficult for them to distinguish between *important* versus *irrelevant* information, since these decisions require judgment skills that are beyond their capabilities. Likewise, their problems

Table 6

Peripheral Supports

- Take notes for student for later review.
- Increase salience of material (e.g., use color coding; increase size of materials).
- Highlight important / relevant information.
- Reduce auditory instructions to writing, and/or provide pictorial forms of support.
- Construct and promote the use of visual supports (e.g., schedules, choice boards, reminder cards, mini schedules, etc.).
- Prepare and monitor use of organizational aids and supports (e.g., checklists, assignment sheets, etc. See additional information under *Self-Management Aids* at the end of this chapter).
- Prepare materials with which to implement teacher-developed lesson plans.
- Develop and employ adaptations to materials when needed.
- Develop concrete templates to sequence the steps in a task.
- Develop routines to maximize student participation and performance.
- Develop and monitor the student's use of rule cards to structure task participation.
- Implement OT, PT, and SLP programs under direction of individual therapists.
- Assume a proactive role in the promotion, monitoring, and use of supports, adaptations, and materials.
- Promote and facilitate student independence and competence in the use of supports.
- Promote and facilitate self-monitoring skills through the use of concrete supports.
- Promote and monitor use of timers to aid performance.
- Keep the teacher informed.
- Seize opportunities to reduce the intrusiveness of peripheral support, where appropriate.
- Anticipate situations in which peripheral support may be needed.
- Read student's signals and behavior.

with organizational skills, which sometimes *erroneously* mask as laziness, *require* standard visual supports such as pictorial or written schedules. Additional organizational and time management supports may be found at the end of this chapter under the heading, *Self-Management Aids.*

Paras and other caregivers typically resist this kind of highly directive support, perhaps because they feel that it goes too far. For neurotypical students, as well as those with disabilities that do not involve deficits in executive function, the support might go too far. This is certainly not the case in autism spectrum disorders. *Students with ASD need certain types of highly directive support if they are to learn the things that their disability precludes them from learning without such assistance.* Try to think of it this way, we would readily recognize the need to take notes for a young man whose arms had been broken, knowing that he couldn't take notes for himself. Why then wouldn't we recognize and acknowledge the need to take notes for a young boy with ASD, knowing that he too can't take notes for himself, albeit for vastly different, though *no less valid* reasons (i.e., because of difficulty determining relevance)? In the first case, the child's problems were *physical.* In the case of ASD, the difficulty is *cognitive.* Likewise, why wouldn't we develop checklists for students to use in monitoring the materials they need for class, when in the absence of these supports their executive function deficits cause them to forget materials, and to be in a constant state of unreadiness? *Bottom Line:* Students with ASD, ADD, and ADHD specifically *require* executive function props (i.e., visual and organizational supports) in order to function more efficiently and effectively.

 Bottom line

The rest of the duties listed in Table 6 are self-explanatory, perhaps with the exception of those related to the implementation of occupational and physical therapy plans (OT and PT, respectively), and those related to speech-language pathology. Occupational therapists will often set up what they call "sensory diets" for students with ASD. These consist of activities that provide relaxation and/or prime the sensory system for some future academic activity. Likewise, physical therapists and speech-language pathologists (SLP's) may set up therapy programs that require implementation by school personnel. Most of the time these programs are most appropriately carried out by paraprofessional support staff. That said, a word of caution is in order.

Therapy plans should be carried out according to the exact specifications of the therapist. If these specifications are not clear (or if the therapist fails to provide adequate direction), *be proactive in seeking out this information.* Ask questions regarding schedule, manner of application, and what to look for vis-à-vis student response. The importance of this cannot be overstated. *When therapy plans are carried out in a haphazard, catch-as-catch-can fashion, they are not only ineffective, but actually do more harm than good.* An example may suffice to drive home this critical point. I once observed a young boy on a brushing program set up by his OT, and implemented by his para. The task was to provide deep pressure sensation at set intervals throughout the day, using a specially designed brush for this purpose. The para in this particular case not only didn't keep to the schedule, but also used light brush strokes which failed to produce the calming sensation which comes from the deep pressure strokes intended by the therapist. The net result was that instead of producing a state of calmness, the procedure made the child more agitated! *Bottom Line:* Just as it is necessary for the para to take direction from the therapist, it is also necessary for the therapist to provide ongoing consultation and monitoring of the student's program, for *it is the therapist's responsibility to make all program modifications and adjustments.* If you feel the need for additional guidance from the therapist, be *proactive* in seeking it out. After all, the *quality* of your work is directly related to the *quality* of the overall direction and supervision you receive from the therapist.

The para's role in the implementation of therapy plans

Bottom line

To summarize, peripheral supports are an important part of educational programming for *all* students with special needs, and an absolute *requirement* for those with ASD. As noted previously, additional ideas and examples for generating these supports may be found at the end of this chapter. Judgments regarding *when, where,* and *how* to use them are part of the "art and science" of paraprofessional support. A strong knowledge base is essential to decision making. Thus, in order to *avoid doing too little* for students with special needs, while at the same time *expecting too much* from them, *it is necessary for you to understand the nature of their deficits.* My premise from the outset has been, *what you don't know may not bother you, but it can jeopardize student learning*—hence, the reason I included the detailed information on autism spectrum disorders in the first seven chapters of this manual, and also urged that you obtain similar information for students with other disabilities, as well. The forms, *Getting To Know Your Student with Special Needs,* and *Learning Style Protocol*, referenced earlier and located at the end of Chapter 8, were specifically designed for this purpose. Such information can guide you in determining what, where and when supports are needed.

Take Home Message

- *Peripheral supports provide crucial supplements* that have the power to *enable* student learning.

- *Visual, organizational, and time management supports are required* to shore up executive function ability in students with ASD, ADD/ADHD, as well as those with other learning disabilities that adversely affect executive function ability.

- *Students with ASD need highly directive support* if they are to learn the things that their disability *precludes* them from learning without support.

- Paras assisting in the implementation of therapy plans should *exercise extreme care in carrying them out according to the therapist's specifications.*

- If it is not forthcoming, *paras should be proactive in seeking continual direction from therapists in the implementation of therapy programs.*

Direct Instruction and Academic Support

There is a great deal of overlap between peripheral supports and direct instruction / academic supports. Table 7 contains a variety of direct supports.

Table 7

Direct Instruction and Academic Supports

- Direct / facilitate attention to teacher, where feasible.
- Direct / facilitate attention to task.
- Assume a proactive role regarding the use of peripheral supports.
- Pre-teach concepts and lessons on a sustained and continuous basis.
- Post-teach concepts and lessons on a sustained and continuous basis.
- Modify task presentation.
- Adjust time requirements.
- Break tasks into smaller units.
- Incorporate student interests to increase motivation.
- Modify teaching style to accommodate student learning style.
- Use interactive story telling technique described in *Social, Play, and Leisure Supports* section of this manual.
- Read student's signals and behavior.
- Prepare supplemental materials and supports to use in the implementation of teacher-developed lessons.
- Anticipate situations in which direct supports may be needed.
- Use repetition, demonstration, and modeling to facilitate performance.
- Use breaks judiciously and bring student up-to-date on material s/he has missed.
- Reinforce student success.
- Facilitate student independence and competence.
- Keep teacher informed.

Facilitating attention

Directing / facilitating attention to the teacher and/or task is at the top of the list of paraprofessional responsibilities involving direct support. More able students—those with mild learning and attentional problems, high functioning autism, and Asperger syndrome—can, under certain circumstances, take in and process information "in the normal course;" that is, as the teacher is presenting it. Some of these circumstances include conditions of low stimulation and/or high interest. What the para needs to do in these situations is to *facilitate the student's attention so that it is directed toward the teacher*.

Less able students are less apt to take in information successfully in the normal course, even under relatively good conditions. In this case, the para needs to *facilitate the student's attention to the task*, rather than to the teacher. In this circumstance, the para needs to take a more *directive* role, with regard to instruction. S/he also needs to assume greater responsibility for utilizing the modifications, adaptations, and supports that are listed in the previous section on *Peripheral Supports,* as they can help to increase the salience of the task and thus promote student attention. It should be obvious that *effective decision-making regarding the selection and use of appropriate supports requires constant vigilance and a keen understanding of the student and his/her specific needs.* This is an extremely important part of the para's responsibilities, since these supports are *necessary* to facilitate student attention, aid understanding, and promote learning.

Pre- and post-teaching are mainstays of direct paraprofessional support for students with significant disabilities, particularly when these students receive most of their education in fast-paced inclusive classrooms. This type of support is particularly critical for students with autism spectrum disorders, since pre-teaching a concept or a lesson enables these students to establish familiarity with the materials and activities *at their own pace, under more controlled conditions* than what is generally available to them in inclusive environments. Similarly, post-teaching not only helps to fortify learning through repetition and practice, but also to promote generalization and maintenance of skills—areas of notorious difficulty in ASD.

Pre-teaching can take place in a quiet area of the regular

Pre- and post-teaching

classroom, a resource room, or a special education classroom. Moreover, pre-teaching can cover a wide variety of topics and activities. For example, at the pre-school and early childhood levels paras can pre-teach nursery rhymes and songs, stories, and specific play sequences well in advance of their presentation in the classroom. Pre-teaching can also encompass physical education activities, concept development, and activities related to any of the academic subjects for both younger and older students. The importance of pre-teaching cannot be overstated, as *it can enable the child to establish a degree of comfort with materials and activities in a less complex, more responsive learning environment.* It also presents students with many more opportunities for repetition and practice than typical children receive, or for that matter, require.

Post-teaching goes hand-in-hand with pre-teaching for all students with special needs, but, as with its counterpart, it is *critical* to the success of those with autism spectrum disorders, given their aforementioned problems with the generalization and maintenance of skills. In other words, it is not enough to present information *only* in advance of lessons. It is also necessary to *re-visit* these same lessons at a later time—in fact, time and time again—since *familiarity breeds attempt* in students with disabilities. Children with ASD, as well as those with other disabilities, benefit from "time in" on tasks if they are to perform well on, or in some cases, even attempt them. In terms of the latter, students with ASD will often avoid tasks that they lack sufficient grounding in, since unfamiliar tasks and activities cause them anxiety and discomfort. (Remember their need for *sameness?!*). Similarly, some students with Asperger syndrome have a proclivity for perfectionism, causing them to avoid participation in activities and tasks until such time as they feel that they can accomplish them perfectly! *Sustained and continuous pre- and post-teaching help to establish a level of comfort with tasks and activities that helps to promote participation.* Furthermore, by continuously "re-cycling" (i.e., *re-visiting*) these activities across people and settings you go a long way toward creating an optimal teaching environment for the generalization and maintenance of skills.

Familiarity breeds attempt!

There are many reasons why students with special needs have difficulty with academic material. One of the more common reasons relates to the way in which the material is presented. For example, a common language arts workbook task consists of directing the student to draw a line from words in the left hand column to those in the right hand column to which they correspond. For some students with special needs the sheer number of words and lines is enough to cause confusion. A *direct instruction modification* might be that of copying each of the words onto index cards and presenting one word at a time (from the left hand column), and only two or three words (from the right hand column) from which the student can select the correct response. A simple modification such as this may mean the difference between performance and nonperformance, or between adequate and substandard performance. In a similar vein, students may have difficulty with taking spelling and other tests with the rest of the class, given the pace and stimulation of the classroom. Paras can provide this type of testing at a reduced pace in a "low stim" environment that can enhance (and in some cases enable!) student performance.

Direct instruction modifications and accommodations

Another accommodation that may be helpful to all students with special needs, particularly those with ASD, is that of breaking down tasks into smaller units so that they do not seem so overwhelming. For example, I once provided consultation on behalf of a young girl named Ashley who reportedly had never finished a math assignment, nor gotten through even part of one without behavioral disruption. Her facial expression at seeing the twelve math problems before her led me to hypothesize that either she didn't like math, and/or the number of examples on the page seemed overwhelming to her. (Her subsequent bolting behavior after a half-hearted attempt at the second problem certainly lent support to my speculation!). The solution, though simple, made a world of difference in the functioning of this student. I recommended that the math assignment be broken down into smaller segments and presented to Ashley at intervals throughout the day—an accommodation that not only lead to successful performance, but also eliminated behavioral disruption.

To summarize, there are countless numbers of adaptations, modifications, and adjustments that can be made to enhance student participation and performance. Some of these relate to the environment or materials that support learning, while others play a more direct role in specific academic programming. For ease of consideration only, I have termed these *peripheral* and *direct academic* supports, respectively. Some supports may be long-standing, as in the case of schedules, timers, and transition symbols. Others may be considered short-term, in the sense of their application in certain, time-limited activities. The language arts example cited above is an example of a short-term support. For the most part, adjustments regarding teaching materials, environment, and instructional style should be planned in conjunction with input from certified staff. The reality, however, is that the paraprofessional support person is often the one to whom this responsibility falls. When this occurs, *it is incumbent upon the para to review the particular adaptation with the teacher so that s/he has the opportunity to evaluate and/or refine the accommodation*.

While there is some "flex" with respect to the above-mentioned supports vis-à-vis teacher involvement, there is no such flexibility regarding curricular modifications. The latter refers to *what to teach* as opposed to *how to teach* (i.e., how to support teaching efforts). Only certified educators can make decisions regarding curricular content; however, these decisions may be *implemented* by paraprofessional support staff under the direction and supervision of the classroom or special subject area teacher. *Bottom line*: Adjustments to the curriculum need to be made by *certified* staff, since such decisions directly affect the *content* of the student's educational program.

Bottom line

Finally, while many types of supports and adjustments may be *pre-planned*, there will always be the need for *on-the-spot decision-making* regarding academic/instructional accommodations. For example, if a science experiment requires dealing with substances that are noxious to the student with special needs, it may be necessary to ask a typical peer to perform the hands-on task for the student, while the student with special needs attends to a more palatable aspect of the project. In some situations, allowing the student to take a break may be all that is necessary to defuse a potentially problematic situation. It is important to note, however, that breaks should be used *judiciously*, since if they are used too frequently, they will likely promote fragmentation in the student's education-

 Bottom line

al program. Moreover, in all cases where breaks are used, it is incumbent upon the para to be *proactive* both in seeking out what the student has missed, and in bringing the student "up to date" after the break. *Bottom Line:* On-the-spot adjustments have their place; however, *their use should not supplant preparation and advanced planning*. If paras rely too heavily on such adjustments, they run the risk of substituting seat-of-your-pants decision-making for thoughtful educational planning. The key here, as in so many other areas, is *balance*.

Take Home Message

- There is a great deal of *overlap* between peripheral and direct instruction / academic supports.

- Effective decision-making regarding the selection and use of appropriate supports requires *constant vigilance* and a *keen understanding* of the student's specific needs.

- Pre- and post-teaching are mainstays of paraprofessional support, and *absolute requirements* in the case of ASD.

- Familiarity breeds *attempt*!

- Modifications / adjustments in task presentation can help to *facilitate* successful performance.

- Adjustments with respect to curricular requirements are within the purview of *certified* staff.

- On-the-spot modifications and adjustments have their place, but *they should not supplant preparation and planning*.

- Breaks should be used *judiciously*, and paras should assume the responsibility for bringing students up to date regarding what they missed.

Social, Play, and Leisure Supports

In many respects, when one enters the realm of social, play, and leisure time supports, one enters uncharted waters. There is a very simple reason for this. Social behavior, play, and leisure skills do not have to be *directly taught* to typical children, for they seem to acquire these skills as if by osmosis. Consequently, there are few guidelines for providing this type of support to students with special needs. Notwithstanding, for children with autism spectrum disorders, in particular, as well as for those with many other types of cognitive impairments, these skills not only have to be directly addressed, but also supported at appropriate times throughout the day.

While social skills programs should be set up, implemented, and monitored by *certified* staff (e.g., school psychologists, speech-language pathologists, social workers, teachers, or school counselors), *paras can nonetheless play a significant role in promoting generalization and maintenance of skills.* Providing planned opportunities for the student to practice specific social behaviors in the cafeteria, playground, or classroom, can help to fortify and generalize skill development. And although it has already been mentioned, it bears repeating here, "free play" situations can be used to *set up* and *facilitate* important social and play behaviors. As always, you need to look for direction from the teacher or other professional staff member regarding program adjustments and refinements. In addition, you need to keep an anecdotal record of student performance. Additional information on this subject is provided later in this chapter under the heading, *Clerical and Record Keeping Responsibilities.* Sometimes social templates are useful for structuring the steps in a complex social or play interaction. When these are used, paras play an important role in monitoring the use of these supports.

The para's role in the generalization and maintenance of skills

There are many supports that can be used for social, play, and leisure skill development. Table 8 contains a listing of some of the more popular techniques. These vary from something as simple as the use of a social cue card to remind the student to appropriately greet his or her speech-language pathologist, or the use of a concrete symbol with the words *My turn* written on it to demarcate the order of turns in a game, to the use of more elaborate techniques.

Table 8

Social, Play, and Leisure Supports

- Use social cue cards to prompt language in social situations.

- Use turn markers for games and sports activities.

- Use environmental "set ups" to promote social and communicative behavior (See *Setting The Individual Up For Communication* at the end of this chapter).

- Use *Social Stories* by Carol Gray.

- Utilize *Story Frames* based upon the work of R. G. Ziegler, M.D.

- Use Opinion Circles.

- Develop and use social templates for structuring the steps in complex social situations.

- Utilize social reminder cards.

- Utilize social rule cards.

- Develop and use social scripts.

- Facilitate interactive behavior with adults and peers.

- Take advantage of "free play" situations by facilitating interactive play behavior.

- Heighten awareness of social information in the environment (See *Ways To "Index" The Environment* at the end of this chapter).

- Read student's signals and behavior.

- Be proactive regarding ways to increase student's involvement in activities and events.

- Promote the generalization and maintenance of social and play behaviors in unstructured environments (e.g., recess, cafeteria, etc.).

- Facilitate student independence and competence.

- Keep the teacher / therapists informed.

- Anticipate situations in which social, play, and leisure supports may be needed.

Setting the Individual Up for Communication! located at the end of this chapter, provides suggestions for ways to promote social and communicative behavior in motivating situations in the natural environment. Suggestions for incorporating neurotypical peers and family members are included. Environmental "set ups" are also excellent vehicles for the generalization and maintenance of skills originally learned in other environments.

Variations on the theme of social supports

Carol Gray has developed a technique known as *Social Stories,* aimed at fostering social understanding in students with ASD, as a means of promoting more appropriate social expression. While this technique was designed for students with autism spectrum disorders, *it is readily applicable to students with other disabilities,* as well. *Social stories* can be written by paras and other caregivers to address specific problem situations. *In order to be effective, however, they must be written according to a specific formula outlined by Ms. Gray.* Writing and implementing social stories is a valid and appropriate use of the para's time, as long as the para is specifically trained to do so. If not, perhaps a teacher can generate a *Social Story* for the para to implement. Information on where to obtain guidelines for writing social stories may be found in Appendix B under the heading *Annotated Resource List.*

A similar technique, and one which requires no particular formula for use, is one that I have termed, *Story Frames.* The idea comes from a book by R.G. Ziegler, M.D. entitled, *Homemade Books to Help Kids Cope.* The reference for this may also be found in Appendix B under the heading *Annotated Resource List.* While the book outlines many uses for this technique, I have used it to provide a visual means of communicating important information to students who have difficulty understanding and processing verbal language. The technique is user-friendly and easy to implement, as Figure 1 clearly indicates. This figure contains an example of a *Story Frame* for helping a child to understand what will happen when he leaves the safe "cocoon" of the resource room to transition into the more complex kindergarten environment.

Figure 1

Story Frame

Bobby and Miss Smith are going to the kindergarten room.

There will be lots of children there.

I can play with the toys.

I can have a snack with the children.

After snack there is circle time.

After circle, Bobby and Miss Smith go back to the learning center.

This tool can also be used as a *direct academic support* for interactive story telling. For example, you can ask the student to direct you to draw items of his/her choosing so that you can develop a story line. You and your student can then take turns telling the story. If you're "stick figure phobic," photographs and magazine cutouts may be used in place of them. For students who are either nonverbal or minimally verbal, you can provide pictures from which they can select subjects, places, and events on which to build a story. For example, if the following pictures are selected—*dog, hot dog, table*—you could put each of the pictures into a different story box and write a story which corresponds to the pictures. Hence, for the order presented above, frame one might say, "This is a dog named Bailey;" frame two: "He is looking at the hot dog on the table;" frame three: "Next, he jumps up and takes the hot dog from the table." To foster critical thinking skills, you could ask the child to *predict* what might happen next, by selecting one picture from the following: a dog eating, and a dog sleeping. Interactive storytelling is also an excellent vehicle for *promoting comprehension, developing narrative skills,* and *pre- and post-teaching* in general. Blank forms for *Story Frames* may be found at the end of this chapter. You needn't confine yourself to six or eight frames, as stories may be shorter or longer depending upon individual circumstances and needs.

Opinion circles can be used to demonstrate the abstract concept of changing one's mind. This one lends itself nicely to the use of neurotypical peers. For example, in making a decision regarding whether to go to MacDonald's or Burger King on the day of the field trip, a blue circle can be used to signify one opinion (MacDonald's), while a yellow circle can be used to signify the other (Burger King). Neurotypical peers can be enlisted to *change their minds* by stepping from one circle to the other, thus demonstrating in a *concrete* manner the *abstract* concept of changing one's mind / opinion.

Additional supports include the use of *social rule cards* to provide students with explicit information in unstructured social situations, such as how to behave in the auditorium or cafeteria. *Social reminder cards* serve a similar, though more discrete purpose. Finally, *social scripts* may be used in role-play situations to practice certain social behaviors. These are particularly useful in pre- and post-teaching activities. All in all, social, play, and leisure supports provide students with *concrete* tools by which to negotiate the many *abstractions* which govern the social world.

Take Home Message

- *Paras play an important role in the generalization and maintenance of social, play, and leisure skills.*

- "Free Play" should be a time when paras *set up and facilitate important social and play behaviors.*

- *Social Stories* and *Story Frames* can help to *increase social understanding as a means of promoting appropriate social expression.*

- *Story Frames* may also be used as a *direct academic support* for interactive story telling.

Behavioral Supports

When you look at behavioral issues in autism spectrum disorders, or in any other disability that causes significant cognitive difficulty, ask yourself the question, *"Which came first?"* ala the chicken or the egg. In the case of ASD there are usually lots of things that come first—*before* behavioral difficulty—such as: the student's inability to understand a situation, activity, or event and the frustration which this causes; the student's extreme discomfort with aversive sensory stimulation; or fatigue, overload, boredom, or some such combination of things that inevitably occurs when one finds oneself in a situation perceived to be irrelevant and/or unmeaningful. Now add to this both the impulsivity that comes from executive function impairment, and the lack of knowledge of appropriate means of responding, and voilà you have a behavior problem—or do you? Not necessarily! What you have in my opinion is a *problem behavior*, not a *behavior problem,* and there is a world of difference between the two.

Problem behaviors are those behaviors that require attention. The caregiver may need to *redirect* the behavior or *substitute*

Problem behaviors vs. behavior problems

a more appropriate response for it. The term *problem behavior* signals the need to work on something. On the other hand, the term *behavior problem* suggests that a value judgment has been rendered and that the student has been found culpable. Think about it. We never hear the phrase, *"Johnny is a problem behavior."* It doesn't even hang together semantically. Conversely, we hear *"Johnny is a behavior problem"* all the time—so much so that, unfortunately, it has an all-too-familiar ring to it.

A good rule of thumb for paras and other caregivers to follow is to adopt the position that a *problem behavior* is *not* the same thing as a *behavior problem*. This statement allows us to *acknowledge and address the problem behavior* without casting the student in the role of *instigator*. There is an educationally sound reason why this distinction is important. If you view Johnny as a *behavior problem* you look no further for behavioral precipitants than within the student himself. In contrast, if you view Johnny as evidencing a *problem behavior,* you are much more likely to look for causes both within *and* outside of him. Table 9 provides a list of important things to consider *before* making precipitous judgments regarding behavior. Careful attention to these issues can enable you to make environmental and other adjustments that can help to prevent *problem behaviors* from becoming *behavior problems.*

When specific behavioral supports are necessary, there are a number of ways to view them. For the purposes of this manual, I have divided them into two categories: *indirect* and *direct.* The former consists of supports designed for *other* purposes, which also prevent or at least minimize behavioral disruption. The latter refer to those that *directly* target problem behaviors. While there is a place for both types of support in the education of students with special needs, it should be obvious that *if indirect supports are used wisely and well, they should go a long way toward minimizing the need for more direct behavioral supports.*

Behavioral supports may be direct or indirect

All of the educational supports that have been outlined in the previous sections of this chapter—those that are either peripheral or direct, as well as those that relate to the development of social, play, and leisure behaviors—may *also* be thought of as *indirect behavioral supports,* since they can help

Table 9

Behavioral Troubleshooting

- Be proactive in scanning the environment for possible behavioral precipitants.

- Reduce or eliminate stressors, to the extent possible.

- Read the student's cues and signals and react *before* inappropriate behavior occurs.

- "Plug in" activities designed to reduce stress and anxiety *before* behavioral disruption occurs (e.g., relaxation exercises, application of deep pressure, etc.).

- Utilize breaks wisely, and only *prior* to behavioral disruption.

- Be *proactive* in providing peripheral, direct academic, and similar supports as preventative behavioral measures.

- Diffuse tense situations through re-direction and distraction, where appropriate.

- Increase structure and predictability.

- Recognize the need for specific behavioral supports.

- Keep the teacher informed of changes in behavior.

 Bottom line

to increase the student's understanding and comfort level, which in turn can help to keep behavior on a more even keel. *Bottom Line:* When students *understand* expectations and tasks, and when they have the *executive function props / organizational supports* to see them through their assignments, there is little need for the anxiety and frustration which fuel behavioral disruption in the absence of these supports. Consequently, the *peripheral*; *direct academic*; and *social, play, and leisure supports* also play an important role in the *prevention* of behavioral difficulty.

Direct behavioral supports, like the name suggests, are those that are implemented in response to specific problem behaviors. Some of these may be thought of as "if - then" supports. In other words, they communicate the following message to the students: *"If you do A, then B will happen,"* where A is the behavior and B is the consequence. For example, *"If you tear up your paper, you will lose your computer time."* In order for if - then supports to be maximally effective, the student must know the target behavior(s) and the consequence(s) in advance.

The Creative Use of Behavior / Learning Contracts

Another type of behavioral support consists of a simple token system type of contract, an example of which is seen in Figure 2.

Figure 2

In this type of contract the child is told that when s/he earns three smiley faces (or tokens), s/he gets to choose an activity of his or her choice. Behavior contracts may be far more elaborate than the simple one depicted above. The adapted contract in Figure 3 was designed for a fourth grade boy with Asperger syndrome by his very creative speech-language pathologist to address the behaviors specified.

There are two major benefits to the type of behavior contract depicted in Figure 3. First, each behavior and consequence is explicitly and clearly specified, enabling the student to fully comprehend what s/he needs to do in order to obtain the reinforcer. Second, the contract is constructed in such a way as to enable the student to *monitor* his or her own behavior. The ability to self-monitor is crucial to the *application* of appro-

Figure 3

Rules for Entering and Leaving Classrooms

1 Be quiet (courtesy)
2 Don't slam the door (courtesy)
3 Sit down, find out what to do (courtesy, efficiency)

I can enter classrooms appropriately.

DATE _____ CLASS _____ STUDENT _____

OBJECTIVE

1. I will enter the room quietly; I will not slam the door.

2. I will sit down at my desk. I will not talk to anyone who is busy.

3a. If I know what to do, I will begin to work immediately and I will follow all regular classroom rules.
OR
3b. If I don't know what to do, I will raise my hand. My teacher will answer me when she has the time. Then I will start to work immediately and follow all rules.

4a. If I have 3 happy faces, I may

_____

OR
4b. If I have any sad faces, I may NOT

_____

Adapted from Mary Jo Chretien. Printed here with permission.

priate behavior in real-life situations.

Some of the most effective behavioral contracts are those that utilize a point system. In this type of contract a specified number of points equates to a specific privilege or other type of reinforcer. The latter may be tangible, as in the case of food or other items, or it may be intangible as in the case of earning points to engage in preferred activities. When using a point system, be sure that the number of points required for the reinforcer is not beyond the student's present ability to comply with the demands of the situation. *Learning new ways of responding takes time and effort.* And although the point was made earlier, it bears repeating here, do not make it virtually impossible for the student to be successful by allowing too much time to elapse between the display of positive behavior and the subsequent reinforcement. The rule of thumb, especially in the early stages, is *short time frames between behavior and reinforcement, with gradually increasing time frames as the student evidences greater ability to control the behavior.* Table 10 provides a list of issues to consider to ensure that the contract system is responsive to student needs.

Table 10

Issues to Consider in Designing Behavior Contracts

The following issues should be brought to the attention of the behavioral support team so that they may be taken into account by the person or persons responsible for designing the behavior contract:

- Match the complexity of the contract to the student's ability level.
- Be creative in both design and choice of reinforcement.
- Monitor effectiveness of the reinforcer, and make changes where appropriate.
- Adjust reinforcement schedule according to the needs of the student.
- Make certain the student understands how the contract works.
- Monitor contract use and make changes / adjustments as appropriate.
- Build in success.
- Facilitate student independence and competence.
- Keep the teacher and behavioral support team informed regarding student progress.

While the actual design of learning / behavioral contracts is beyond the scope of this manual, a "word to the wise" is in order. These contracts require understanding of the principles of behavior modification. As such, they are best addressed by the educational team. Behavior specialists—if you have the luxury of having access to one—can be of immeasurable value in the design and implementation of learning / behavioral contracts. If not, certified staff often have a good deal of experience in this area. The important thing to remember is that *poorly designed learning/behavior contracts provide poor behavioral support. Bottom line*: Contracts, if used wisely and well, can provide students with special needs with a *meaningful incentive for positive behavioral change.* For students with autism spectrum disorders behavior contracts not only provide an important incentive, but also a "road map" for understanding and negotiating the enigmatic social world so that they can act in ways that make the things that are important to them happen in their lives.

💡 Bottom line

Before leaving the subject of behavioral support, a cautionary statement is in order:

BE SURE THAT YOU DO NOT *INADVERTENTLY* REINFORCE INAPPROPRIATE BEHAVIOR!

💡 Analyze the function the behavior serves

Students act out for different reasons. Sometimes students act out to get out of situations which they find uncomfortable, or worse yet, aversive. The example cited earlier of the student who threw the art project off the desk because s/he found the glue aversive is an example of this. Other students act out because they don't understand what is going on and do not want to remain in situations that are meaningless to them. In both of these cases, *the students act out to get out!* To wit, please consider the plight of Agnosia—a situation which Charles Hart and I contrived, and which he expertly depicted. Figure 4 illustrates the world according to Agnosia, which from *her* perspective is nothing more than *Little Aggie and the Babbling Monsters:*

Figure 4

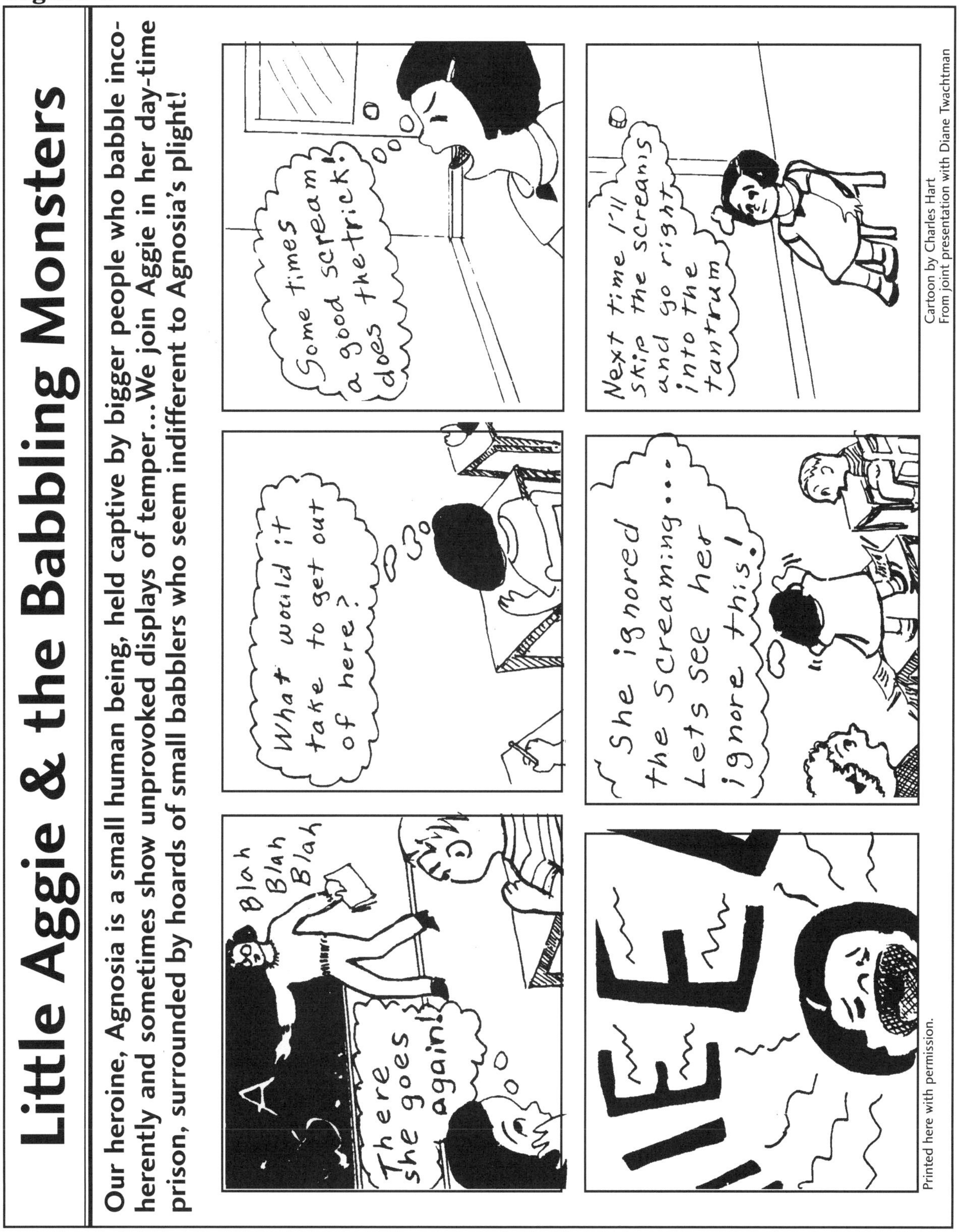

Little Aggie & the Babbling Monsters

Our heroine, Agnosia is a small human being, held captive by bigger people who babble incoherently and sometimes show unprovoked displays of temper....We join Aggie in her day-time prison, surrounded by hoards of small babblers who seem indifferent to Agnosia's plight!

Cartoon by Charles Hart
From joint presentation with Diane Twachtman

Printed here with permission.

Important rule
of thumb

It should be obvious that Aggie's acting out behavior is the result of her lack of understanding of the teacher (i.e., the "it's all *Greek* to me" phenomenon!). Uncomfortable in such a situation, she *acts out* in order to *get out* of the classroom. From the smile on her face and the look of relief, it is clear that she got exactly what she wanted when she was removed from the classroom and put into time out. *Rule of thumb: If the student acts out to get out, and gets out, you have reinforced (albeit inadvertently) the aberrant behavior!* If, however, the student acts out to *obtain* your attention, *time out* may be exactly what s/he needs to learn the following: That's not the way to get the adult's attention! Table 11, *Maxims of Behavioral Intervention,* contains important information vis-à-vis behavior for you to keep in mind.

Table 11

Maxims of Behavioral Intervention

- If the student acts out to get out, and s/he gets out (i.e., is removed from the room and/or placed in time out), you have inadvertently *reinforced* the behavior.

- If the student acts out specifically to get your attention, removal from the room / time out is an appropriate option.

- There is a clear and definitive difference between *behavior management* and *behavior modification*, in that the former implies control, and the latter implies change.

- While behavior management (*control*) can be an appropriate short-term strategy, behavior modification (*change*) is the most appropriate long-term goal.

- Problem behaviors are *not* the same as behavior problems!

Being a realist—how could I be otherwise with the amount of time I spend in classrooms—I am well aware that there are times when the student must be removed from the classroom, even if such removal is reinforcing to him or her at the time. Typical peers have just as much right to a "free appropriate public education" as their classmates with special needs. If the latters' behavior is so disruptive as to interfere with the education of their classmates, they must be temporarily removed from the classroom so that they may gain control of their behavior. I consider this to be a *short-term behavioral strategy to address a problem* (i.e., behavior *management*), rather than a *long-term behavioral solution to bring about change* (i.e., behavior *modification*). The former may, at times, be necessary. But, generally speaking, *behavior management should not be used as a long-term strategy,* since it does not teach the student *new* ways of responding, but rather merely *manages* the immediate situation. Behavior *modification,* on the other hand, implies *change.* When short-term behavior management strategies are necessary, it is essential that a team meeting be called so that *all* aspects of the situation may be discussed and *long-term* strategies implemented. To aid that discussion, soon after the behavioral occurrence, the form entitled, *Guidelines for the Analysis of Problem Behavior,* located at the end of this chapter, should be filled out by the person closest to the student at the time of the incident. As trench person extraordinaire, that duty usually falls to you. Hopefully the above-noted form can help you to accomplish your mission.

💡 Behavior management vs. behavior modification

To summarize, behavioral issues loom large in autism spectrum disorders, given both the students' difficulty dealing with the demands of an enigmatic and rapidly moving social world, and the tendency of even the most *well-intentioned* caregivers to misconstrue their students' actions and to deem the behaviors in question as intentional and willful. Behavioral difficulty is also common in other disorders in which problems in cognition impede understanding and cause frustration and anxiety. Your role as a para in this behavioral minefield is somewhat sketchy. In other words, because of your proximity to the student, you often bear the brunt of the behaviors, both literally and figuratively! Even so, you don't have a "free hand" in determining consequences. *Situations involving behavioral excesses require team input,* for two or more heads really are better than one when it comes to analyzing behavior and generating hypotheses on which to base solutions. But you are a valuable and integral part of the student's educational team, given your front and center proximity to the student. Your role is to step up to the plate in the behavior analysis phase, and when a behavioral strategy has been determined by the team, to retire to the outfield with the

💡 The importance of teamwork

rest of the players to support the team's decision.

Take Home Message

- Always ask yourself the question, *"Which came first, the behavior or some frustrating or aversive situation that may have caused it?"*

- *Problem behaviors* are not the same as *behavior problems*.

- Behavioral supports may serve an *indirect* or *direct* function.

- The wise use of *indirect* supports can *minimize,* and in some cases *eliminate* the need for more direct supports.

- By exercising *vigilance*, it is possible to prevent *problem behaviors* from becoming *behavior problems*.

- Academic, social, play, and leisure supports may help to *prevent* behavioral disruption.

- Learning / behavior contracts provide students with ASD with a *"road map"* for understanding and negotiating the complex social world.

- Exercise extreme care so as not to *inadvertently* reinforce inappropriate behavior.

- *Behavior management provides a short-term strategy* to handle a problem, whereas *behavior modification promotes long-term change*.

- Situations involving behavioral difficulty require *team input*.

Clerical and Record Keeping Responsibilities

Table 12 lists the all-important (but never enthusiastically welcomed) clerical tasks that provide a written record of the student's day-to-day functioning. No mere busy work, these record keeping activities are an *integral* part of the student's programming, providing caregivers with important information regarding *progress*, *setbacks*, and a *road map for future planning*. This information also serves an important *accountability* function. While most of the clerical / record keeping tasks are self-explanatory, a few require additional elaboration. The *Collaborative Consultation Implementation Plan (CCIP)* and the *Buddy Networks Observation System (BNOS)*, located at the end of this chapter, are two data sheets that will enable you to look at the *qualitative* aspects of social, communicative, and play behaviors in your students. They should be shared with the professional staff responsible for setting up social, play, and leisure skill activities so that these record keeping forms may be used to full advantage in the implementation of their programs. The type of information which these data sheets provide is extremely valuable, since progress with respect to social, communicative, and play behaviors is notoriously difficult to document, given that all of these skills are multidimensional, highly dependent upon context, and not well-served by simple percentages. The *CCIP* and *BNOS* can also provide an important vehicle for promoting and charting progress in the generalization and maintenance of skills.

The goal of record keeping

Some situations lend themselves to the keeping of *quantitative* data. This is most often reported in the form of percentages. Just be careful that the specific behavior you're reporting in such form really lends itself to percentages, and/or that the percentages actually make sense. In terms of the former, I am reminded of the following IEP entry: *Johnny will complete the art project with 70% accuracy*. Judging the percentage of completion of an art project is an "art form" of which few are capable! In terms of what I call *silly* percentages, consider the following example: *Johnny will cross the street safely 4 out of 5 times*. Conceivably, Johnny could achieve this objective with 80% accuracy (an honorable percentage by anyone's standard) and still meet with disaster on the fifth trial! Some things just don't lend themselves to percentages. When they do, by all means report the data in that form. When they don't, try to record the behavior in a more *meaningful* manner. The qualitative data sheets at the end of this chapter are one way to accomplish this. Others might include the use of checklists, matrices, progress logs, and similar tools.

Beware of silly percentages

Table 12

Clerical and Record Keeping Responsibilities

- Record information on *CCIP* and *BNOS* forms. (See forms at the end of this chapter).

- Develop and use additional anecdotal record forms to record qualitative aspects of social, communicative, and play / leisure behaviors, where appropriate.

- Record quantitative data for activities and tasks for which that type of information is meaningful.

- Utilize checklists for organizational support and for charting progress.

- Utilize matrices and graphs for information that is best reported in these formats.

- Keep progress logs, where appropriate.

- Develop a *Para's Log Book* to record observations, and to keep track of promising / not-so-promising practices.

- Record information on *Input for Student Planning Meeting* form. (See form at the end of this chapter).

- Be proactive and vigilant regarding use of the *Special Subject Area Request* form. (See form at the end of this chapter).

- Share information with the classroom teacher at regular intervals.

- Be proactive in seeking out information and keeping records regarding IEP goals and objectives.

- Keep records regarding any increase or decrease in problem behavior(s), and bring to the attention of the teacher / behavioral support team.

- Monitor student's use of various supports.

- Monitor use and type of prompts.

- Exercise vigilance in fading back prompts. (See Table 13, Chapter 10, for explanation and use of the *Transactional Interaction Model for Educational and Behavioral Support (TIM)* designed for this purpose).

- Keep track of problems, setbacks, progress, and needs of student, and keep the teacher fully informed.

- Perform clerical duties, as assigned by teachers.

The *Para's Log Book* is your "stream of consciousness"—reflections from the person in the trenches! Your proximity to your students gives you an enviable vantage point. Entries should be made on a daily basis, but they need not be lengthy, nor rendered in exquisite prose. The log book is not intended to house detailed descriptions of each day, but rather to encapsulate the most *salient* aspects of the day vis-à-vis your student's functioning. Consider the sample entry which follows:

Susan had a very good day, particularly with respect to peer interaction. With moderate support, she was able to sustain two separate playground interactions—one involving the sand box, and one involving the seesaw—for approximately seven minutes each. Use of organizational aids (i.e., checklists) still requires adult prompting, but are very effective in helping her to manage her belongings.

This log book should also contain a separate section entitled, *Promising/Not-So-Promising Practices*. This section should house your stream of consciousness regarding what works, and equally as important, what doesn't work. Sample entries for promising practices might include:

Use of color coding enables Susan to keep main characters separate from secondary characters (e.g., main in yellow; secondary in blue).

Use of a "sticky" note reminder to "raise your hand" works like a charm!

Sample entries for not-so-promising practices might include:

No wonder the behavior contract didn't work. I just found out Susan doesn't like M&M's!

Requiring Susan to speak in complete sentences causes her a great deal of frustration.

The importance of including this type of information should not be taken lightly. For one thing, it provides a record for IEP and other meetings. For another, it provides information for the next teacher and para (in the event you are re-assigned or decide to leave) of what works and what doesn't work. The log book also enables you to keep track of the adaptations and modifications which you've put into place during the year. That way, no one, including you, has to "re-discover" the techniques and practices that enable learning next year! Finally, the log book also serves an important accountability function.

Another crucial piece of information that you and you alone can supply is your very own input regarding student functioning. Ideally, you should be present at all planning meetings involving your student. In reality, there are many school districts where this doesn't happen, since many teachers and administrators deem it more important for you to be in the classroom with the student. Even when you are given release time to attend meetings, the amount of time you are given is often insufficient for you to have more than cursory involvement. The form entitled *Input for Student Planning Meeting* should be filled out in advance of all meetings, *whether or not you are able to attend*, as it will provide a written record of salient information about the student. If you are able to attend the planning meeting, the information can help to focus your comments. In either case, the document provides a vehicle for your important input. This form may be found at the end of this chapter.

Be proactive in seeking out the information you need

Finally, given your proximity to the student, and your close monitoring of all aspects of his or her functioning, much of the job of day-to-day record keeping is one that must necessarily fall to you. In many respects, you are the "common denominator" in the student's school life—the person who is not only with him or her in the inclusive or special education classroom, but also, to some extent, in all other settings as well (e.g., resource room, art, music, physical education, cafeteria, and recess). The support you provide in these unstructured settings can spell the difference between success and failure for the student. For this reason, you need to be *proactive* in seeking out much needed information on which to base your accommodations. The *Special Subject Area Request* form located at the end of this chapter is useful for obtaining advanced notice regarding the content of lessons and activities. This form can be placed in each teacher's mailbox in advance of classes. The information they provide can enable you to prepare educational supports in advance, and/or to otherwise modify materials or task presentation. Moreover, such knowledge can also enable you to provide pre-teaching activities for the student to increase familiarity and comfort level vis-à-vis upcoming lessons. It is important to note that individual teachers will differ on whether to assign you additional record keeping tasks such as writing in the home-school communication book. Consequently, responsibility for these activities will vary from setting to setting.

Whatever the extent of your record keeping, three points are in order: 1) Be vigilant—*haphazard, sloppy record keeping compromises student learning.* 2) *Share the information with the classroom teacher at regular intervals,* for it is up to him or her to use such information to make educational decisions. 3) If the teacher doesn't provide you with your student's IEP goals and objectives, *be proactive in seeking them out.* After all, what you don't know (about the goals and objectives) you can neither address, monitor, nor keep data on!

Three critical points

Take Home Message

- Record keeping activities are an *integral* part of the student's programming, providing important information regarding *progress, setbacks,* and *a road map for future planning.*

- There is a place for both *qualitative* and *quantitative* data.

- Be *proactive* in seeking out the information you need regarding *IEP goals* and *objectives,* and the *content* of lessons and activities.

- Haphazard, sloppy record keeping *compromises* student learning.

- *Share information* with the classroom, special education, and special area teachers at regular intervals.

To summarize, it can truly by said of all of the supports addressed in this section of the manual that each one serves an important and *multifaceted* purpose. At a minimum, they help to:

- promote understanding

- increase stability

- minimize anxiety and discomfort

- aid information processing

- shore up executive function ability

- provide cues for performance

- exert a positive influence on behavior

- enhance social, play, and leisure skill development

- promote independence and competence

- enhance overall student learning

It should be obvious that, without support, students with disabilities are left to fend for themselves without the "prerequisite skills" for taking in and dealing with the information coming at them. Under such circumstances, stress and anxiety increase and learning is compromised. Hence, it is incumbent upon paraprofessional support staff to do whatever it takes to *support* student learning.

Bottom line

Chapter 11 contains sample modifications and examples of visual and organizational supports presented in a "how to" vignette format, so as to provide you with a blueprint for applying the types of educational supports discussed in this chapter. The examples selected address problems commonly encountered in the education of students with disabilities, and the format in which they are rendered provides a user-friendly template (i.e., formula) for coming up with solutions to your own problem situations. *Bottom Line:* educational supports are an *essential* part of programming for students with special needs. To put these supports in perspective, they should be considered *educational prostheses* in much the same way as physical prostheses such as eyeglasses aid vision, and crutches aid walking. We would not withhold necessary prosthetic devices from those who need them. Let us not withhold educational prostheses from students with special needs, since their use can mean the difference between success and failure.

Take Home Message

- *Special* education *requires* the use of *specialized* educational supports!

- Paras need to assume a *proactive* role in the use of educational supports for students with special needs.

Self-Management Aids (SMA's)

Self-Management Aids are tools which enable people with organizational problems to keep track of information, and to deal with it more effectively and efficiently. Students with ASD and ADD/ADHD have well-known difficulty with organization and planning. Moreover, organizational and planning ability decrease as environments become more complex and demanding.

The SMA's which follow are visually-based supports designed to provide stability and consistency regarding information intake, management, and disposition. They are as essential to individuals with organizational problems as eyeglasses and hearing aids are to the visually and auditorally impaired, respectively.

- **Schedule:** A daily schedule is an essential management aid for students with organizational problems. It helps them to establish clear beginning and ending points for activities; to anticipate future events; and to develop a better sense of time, overall. In addition, a daily schedule helps to build in consistency and predictability. Used with a transition and/or change symbol, schedules can also enable students to better understand and anticipate change. This can go a long way toward minimizing transition difficulty.

Task Organizers (TO's)

- **Assignment Folders:** These may be incorporated into a loose-leaf notebook. There are two types that work well for students with organizational problems:

    - **Two-pocket file folders**—Mark the left side **WORK TO DO**. Mark the right side **FINISHED**. These folders may be color-coded for each subject.

    - **Traditional file folders**—These may be used for specific assignments. For example, under the Language Arts section of the loose-leaf notebook, spelling work may be kept in a blue file folder; compositions in a yellow folder.

    - **Assignment Sheets:** These can help students to keep track of assignment due dates, and what to do with the finished product.

    - **Planning Charts:** These can be used to structure tasks that are to be completed over a long period of time. A planning calendar can be used in conjunction with this chart. For example, if the assignment is a term paper due in four weeks, each of the weeks can be broken down into mini assignments such as: **Week 1**–Obtain book from library and read; **Week 2**–Collect facts from internet / encyclopedia, etc.; **Week 3**–Write rough draft; **Week 4**–Edit draft and write final report.

    - **Calendar Systems**: Blank, monthly calendar sheets with large spaces can be duplicated, so that the student has a visual representation of daily activities over a month-long period. As noted above, these can be used in conjunction with other discrete task organizers.

Self-Management Aids (SMA's)
Page 2

Assignment Organizers (AO's)

- These may be used to structure multi-step tasks to enable the student to "chain through" steps in an organized, sequential manner. For example, an AO for a science class might contain the following: a box that contains the list of materials for the project; the list of sequential steps needed to complete the project; a box containing instructions for disposition of the project; and a place to check-off that the work has been completed.

MISCELLANEOUS SELF-MANAGEMENT AIDS

Rule Cards (RC's)

- These serve as reminders with respect to classroom behavior. They help the student keep important rules of conduct in mind regarding participation in class activities. These cards may be kept in a small loose-leaf binder with index tabs to allow for easy reference.

- **Checklists:** These can be used to remind the student of materials to take to the next class, and/or materials to take home at the end of the day. Checklists can also be used to help students "chain through" the steps in a multi-step task.

- **"Sticky" Notes:** These can be used as quick and easy on-the-spot reminders. They come in a variety of colors and sizes, and as such, may be "coded" accordingly. For example, if the student has difficulty remembering to raise his/her hand, a "sticky" note reminder can help to keep the information "on-line".

- **Color-Coded Self-Adhesive Circles:** These may be used to signify such things as the following:

  Yellow: Important/Immediate

  Blue: Not Urgent

- **Index Tabs** to allow easy access to materials

- **Cue Cards** to serve as stable, visual reminders of important information (e.g., Ask for help if you don't understand.).

Self-Management Aids (SMA's)
Page 3

Personal Space Organizers (PSO's)

- An **organizational "grid"** for the desk or similar space can help students keep school papers and other materials organized. For example, glue together the following boxes: a shirt box; a necklace box; a tie box; and assorted square and rectangle boxes
    Label each one as follows:

    - (shirt box) papers

    - (necklace box) pencils / pens

    - (tie box) rulers, etc.

    - (assorted boxes) erasers, paper clips, elastics, etc.

- **Plastic file holders** to house work-in-progress and completed assignments

- **Holders of various types / sizes** to house the items noted above and/or other materials (e.g., boxes, baskets, cylinders, and other containers).

Note: The Self-Management Aids listed here are but a few of the many tools available to students with ASD and other disorders that create problems in organization and planning. Similar supports can be generated, as needed, by support staff working with these students.

The most important aspect of these visual supports is that they enable students to function with greater independence and competence, and with less anxiety.

IMPORTANT REMINDER REGARDING STUDENTS WITH ORGANIZATIONAL PROBLEMS:

Extra time and effort should be taken to ensure that directions are clear and understandable to the student. As such,

- They should not be too "wordy."

- They should be written down or accompanied by visual supports, particularly when they involve multiple steps.

- They should not consist of figurative language.

- They should be accompanied by examples, and demonstration and modeling, where appropriate.

- There should be assurances that the student has understood the directions.

Setting the Individual Up for Communication!

Environmental Set-Ups for Context-Based Pragmatic Intervention

Inducements designed to promote the idea of communication as a vehicle for *social interaction* provide powerful tools to *control* one's world. *Observation* and *timing* are extremely important; that is, the key to getting the most out of this technique is to *observe* the individual with ASD closely, and provide the prompt *before* frustration occurs. Activities are suitable, with adaptations, for all age levels, provided age-appropriate materials are used.

1. Have a neurotypical peer walk into the room with a *preferred* food item or object. When the student with ASD sees the item, have the peer *immediately* prompt, "Call Ms. Doe." "Say, want (food item / object)."

Pragmatic skills targeted: accessing; requesting.

2. Stage problem solving situations in which the student needs to request specific items in order to carry out a task / activity. For example, give him/her a bowl of soup without a spoon and prompt him/her to request spoon. Hide one of his/her shoes and say, "What do you need?" Or, put a preferred item in an unexpected and inaccessible place and prompt him/her to ask for it: "Cookie?"

Pragmatic skills targeted: requesting; answering (if adult asks question); questioning; seeking information and/or help.

3. Use objects or pictures as cues (i.e., "triggers") for requests. For example, if the student prefers to go to a particular place, have a picture of it available so that s/he can hand it to you to request going there. (Have these cues available *only* if the request can be granted).

Pragmatic skills targeted: requesting; asking permission; informing; accessing (if individual brings the picture to you).

4. Set up obstacles to block desired objects and activities. Prompt the student to *do* or *say* something to make things happen. For example, give him/her a small container of M&M's that cannot be opened. Prompt, "Help me." Or, have a classmate stand in front of the video screen while the student is watching something, and prompt him/her to say, "Move."

Pragmatic skills targeted: directing; ordering; requesting; controlling.

Setting the Individual Up for Communication!
Page 2

5. Give the student only a small portion of something so that s/he has to request more.

Pragmatic skill targeted: requesting.

6. Offer *choices* of snack food, beverages, vegetables, places to go, clothing, etc. *whenever possible*, so that the student can use language to *select* the things that are important to him/her.

Pragmatic skills targeted: requesting; informing; directing; controlling; possibly accessing.

7. Offer the student items you know s/he does *not* like and prompt him/her to reject them saying, "Tell me, no." Or, shake head or sign no, as less intrusive prompts.

Pragmatic skills targeted: refusing; rejecting; protesting; controlling; directing.

8. Be alert to situations, events, and/or activities that the student finds boring or uncomfortable. Watch reaction carefully and prompt him/her to say such things as, "Want to stop!", "Need a break", or "Finished".

Pragmatic skills targeted: directing; controlling; informing; requesting; protesting.

9. Use an object in an unusual manner. For example, run a Match Box Car upside down or comb hair with wrong side of comb. Have a third party (classmate or teacher) point out situation and model appropriate response.

Pragmatic skills targeted: commenting; informing. Directing, ordering, or controlling - if student tries to change situation.

10. Withhold a turn in a *preferred* activity. Use gesture of hand on chest to model / say, "My turn." Put the student's hand on his/her own chest, model / say, "Bobby's turn". Or, suddenly stop a movement pattern, like bouncing on a trampoline, and encourage the student to indicate desire for continuation of activity (i.e., "More").

Pragmatic skills targeted: requesting; informing.

Ways to "Index" the Environment

The following cueing strategies enable paras and other caregivers to point out important information that students with special needs might otherwise miss.

1. Point out *social* information:
   "Look, Timmy's waving at you. Can you wave back?"

2. Point out *emotional* information:
   "Mary got hurt. Look, she's crying. Poor Mary. Can you tell Mary, 'I'm sorry'?"

3. Point out *anticipatory* information:
   "Look, Joey's going to throw the ball. Put your hands up."

4. Structure the *commenting* function:
   "Look at the bird eating the bird seed. The bird must be hungry."

5. Code *feelings* and *reactions*:
   "Ryan's very angry at Joey for taking that ball. Tell Joey, 'give me that ball.'"

6. Encourage *perspective-taking*:
   "Ryan *likes* his pickle. Look, Joey *hates* his pickle. Look at Joey. Joey's making a face that says, 'I *hate* this pickle.'"

From: Twachtman, D.D. (1995). Methods to Enhance Communication in Verbal Children. In K.A.Quill (Ed.), *Teaching Children with Autism: Strategies to Enhance Communication and Socialization* (pp. 133-162). Albany, NY: Delmar. Reprinted with permission of Delmar, a division of Thomas Learning.

Story Frame

Story Frame

Guidelines for the Analysis of Problem Behavior

This instrument requires input from certified staff if it is to be used effectively as a tool for analyzing behavior and rendering judgments.

Name of Student: **Date:**

Description of problem behavior:

Circumstances preceding, and events surrounding problem behavior:

Immediate management strategy:

Problem Solving Guide

Please rate the following parameters operating *at the time* of the behavioral occurrence. Circle the answer that applies best. In some cases, more than one answer may apply. Leave blank if unable to render a judgment.

• General use of visual supports (e.g. transition markers; schedule; choice board, etc.)	high / low / non-existent
• Visual supplementation vis-à-vis task presentation	high / moderate / low / non-existent
• Degree of auditory load	high / moderate / low
• Presence of environmental stressors	high activity level / excessive noise / large number of people / distractions
• Degree of environmental structure	high / moderate / low
• Student's familiarity with task	high / moderate / low
• Presentation of task	in context / out of context / too little information given
• Opportunities for "hands on"	high / moderate / low / non-existent
• Degree of abstractness of task	high / moderate / low
• Complexity of language load	high / moderate / low
• Sensory issues	avoidant behavior / seeking behavior / other (specify)
• Motor planning issues	N/A / interfering (specify)
• Attentional behavior during task / activity	high / moderate / low / perseverative / intermittent

Guidelines for the Analysis of Problem Behavior
Page 2

- General distractibility index   high / moderate / low

- Use of demonstration/modeling   high / moderate / low / non-existent

- Use of prompts   high / moderate / low

- Types of prompts used   verbal / visual / physical / combination

- Composition of environment (re: noise, number of
  people / activities)   simple / complex

- Predictability of environment   highly predictable / unpredictable

- Use of reinforcers (specify)   high / low / non-existent

- Benefit of reinforcement   high / low / non-existent

- Reinforcement schedule   too much time between stimulus & reinforcer

Areas to Consider

Please circle those which may apply:

I. Possible contributory factors:
    - medication change
    - fatigue
    - lack of sleep
    - dietary change
    - physical illness
    - internal factors
    - change in home situation
    - seizure activity
    - environmental
    - other (specify)

II. Signs of stress preceding problem behavior (list):

III. Hypothesis regarding the communicative function served by the behavior:

IV. Behavior Modification Action Plan (B-MAP): (List steps to take to address the problem):

Collaborative Consultation Implementation Plan (CCIP)

Date:

Student: _____

Classroom: _____

GENERALIZATION DESIGN

Communication/ Language Targets	Contexts/ Activities	Socialization Opportunities	Supports/ Prompts	Comments

Buddy Network Observation System (BNOS)

Student: _____   Date: [   ]

Peer Participants: _____

OBSERVATION PROTOCOL

Play/Socialization Goal	Contexts/ Activities	Props/ Materials	Supports/ Prompts	Comments

Input for Student Planning Meeting

Date:

Student:

Respondent:

I.   Overview of Student Behavior Since Last Meeting

II. Documentation Regarding Areas of Progress

III. Documentation Regarding Problem Areas / Setbacks

IV. Factors Related to Progress and Setbacks

V.   Description of Educational Supports in Use

VI. Student Strengths, Weaknesses, and Needs

VII. Additional Considerations

VIII. Action Plan (To be generated at student planning meeting)

Special Subject Area Request

To:

From:

Student's Name:

Please provide information regarding the following topics to assist me in preparing an assignment organizer, and in pre-teaching, and/or preparing templates, checklists, and other supports to assist the above-named student in your class.

1. **Overview of the Planned Lesson / Activity:**

2. **Specifics Regarding Expectations for Student Participation / Performance:**

3. **Materials Required:**

4. **Recommendations Regarding Supports and Pre-teaching Activities / Materials:**

5. **Additional Information Regarding Ways to Assist Student:**

Chapter Ten

You're in the Trenches Now
The "Art" of Being a Para Pro

"Science" can exist without "art" in the rendering of support to students with special needs. By this is meant that it is possible to be an excellent technician regarding the implementation of the supports discussed in the last chapter. This may suffice if *all* goes well *all* the time—a tall order, to say the least! Problems ensue when unexpected things happen (as they invariably do), for these require artful analysis and sound judgment, both of which go significantly beyond simple science. An example may serve both to drive home the important distinction between "science" and "art," and to set the stage for considering their place in paraprofessional support.

Individuals who lack a fundamental understanding of computers can nonetheless, with training, be taught to be fairly proficient in using them for specified purposes. This is especially true when the computer activity is relatively simple and repetitive. As long as things remain copacetic (i.e., proceed according to expectation) all is fine. If, however, a computer operator with marginal understanding of computers inadvertently hits the wrong key, causing what for him or her is an inexplicable consequence (complete with indecipherable on-screen "instructions"), the narrow, decompartmentalized knowledge required to perform the repetitive computer activity won't go very far in helping the individual to troubleshoot or remediate the situation. In other words, *technical knowledge—or the "science"—can take you only so far.* It won't help you to handle problems when they arise, nor will it enable you to branch out and be creative. The reason for this is quite straightforward. *Technical "proficiency", without true under-*

The importance of blending art with science

standing leaves you with "no moves to make" when something unforseen happens.

Now consider the case of a highly skilled, computer-literate individual who has a fundamental and flexible understanding of the computer, and the myriad ways in which it can be used. When glitches occur, the individual's broad-based understanding enables him or her to independently think the problem through and to figure out which keys to hit in order to correct it. Moreover, the computer-literate individual has no difficulty venturing forth to explore new ways of using the computer creatively. The difference between this individual and the one noted earlier, is that in the present example the more knowledgeable, computer-literate person has mastered both the "art" *and* "science" of computers. As such, not only does s/he have many moves to make when things go wrong, s/he can also engage in effective troubleshooting, and exercise creativity in job performance.

This analogy applies equally well to the art and science of paraprofessional support for, if the truth be known, it is not enough for paras to master *either* the art *or* the science of paraprofessional support. Either - or just won't do. Rather, a blend of *both* art and science is required in the educational care of students with special needs, particularly if you are striving to be a para *pro* at what you do. Before considering ways to go about this, it is worthwhile to first look at things to avoid. *Enter the problem para!*

The next few pages contain tongue-in-cheek examples of serious errors made by paraprofessional support staff. Though some may seem contrived, please be assured that I have encountered all of these problem para prototypes more often than I'd like to think. With some exceptions, which I will point out, most of these problem situations occur because of lack of knowledge and/or training—deficiencies which I hope this manual will go a long way toward remediating. Others, however, are the result of attitudinal deficiencies which are more insidious and hence more difficult to confront and correct. So, as you peruse the *Problem Para Parodies,* it's okay to unleash your sense of humor, but don't let it run wild, for there are lessons to be learned in your mission to become a para *pro*! Enter the *Space Cadet Para* in Figure 5.

Figure 5

The Space Cadet Para

Lost in Space

These problem paras are truly lost in space, with no clues as to what their students need, nor how to provide support. They move about classrooms as though ensconced in their personal space suits, isolated from not only the students to whom they've been assigned, but also from the classroom culture which they never quite grasp. In their rarefied atmosphere they make no mental contact with the duties and responsibilities of their jobs, relying upon classroom teachers for virtually all direction regarding activities and supports. More maddening, however, is their utter lack of common sense and logic with respect to following directives and recommendations. I encountered one such para a few years ago. I explained the importance of using a visual schedule so that her kindergarten student could come to understand how his day was to unfold. A picture depicting each classroom activity was to be Velcroed onto a board so that the child could check his schedule at the beginning of an activity, and then remove the picture and place it in a "finished" box when the activity ended. Such a schedule, I explained, would establish clear beginnings and clear endings for the child, thus ameliorating, if not eliminating his transition difficulty. It took three visits over several months—*each one to address the same transition-related problem*—before I prevailed upon this para to actually carry out my recommendation. When she finally acquiesced, she placed the schedule several feet above the student's eye level, which sadly ended up not mattering, since she never even consulted the schedule either before or after activities, thereby negating the very reason it had been recommended in the first place. Another "spacey" para used her mother's good china for a "Little Miss Muffet" sequence involving a preschool child, with predictably "shattering" results. (Did I have to specify plastic, and wasn't I lucky that she didn't use a real spider!?). The sad but true story is that *with the Space Cadet Para you do have to specify the obvious,* for these paras are so oblivious to their students' needs, and so lacking in common sense that they are likely to interpret the adage, *follow the student's lead* quite literally—as in onto a busy thoroughfare!

Bottom line

Bottom Line: Space Cadet Paras just don't get it! As such, they are part of the problem rather than the solution. Worse yet, the Space Cadet Para's lack of such "earthly phenomena" as common sense and good judgment is not only inimical to student learning, but also potentially dangerous to student well-being. Enter, the *Parrot Para,* in Figure 6.

Figure 6

The Parrot Para

This type of problem para quite literally *repeats* everything the teacher says to the class, as in the following sequence:

Teacher: "Take out your books."

Parrot Para: "Take out your book."

Teacher: "Turn to page 40."

Parrot Para: "Turn to page 40."

Teacher: "Do examples 1-10."

Parrot Para: "Do examples 1-10."

If all the student with special needs requires is repetition, then the school district could save a fair amount of money by eliminating this para's position and requiring the teacher to either say each directive twice, or utilize a tape recorder for this purpose. Besides, if the student has an autism spectrum disorder, the last thing he or she needs is an *echolalic* para (i.e., one who echoes everything that has been said)!

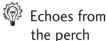
Echoes from the perch

Rarely will simple repetition be all that is needed to facilitate the student's attention or participation. If, as noted earlier in this manual, under high interest / "low stim" conditions the student can take in information in the normal course—as long as there is repetition and sufficient "wait" time—then s/he can best be served by the para facilitating attention to the teacher, rather than the para's merely repeating what the latter has just said. Hence, the following is a far more appropriate use of the para's (and the student's) time: *"Susan, Mr. Smith is speaking to you. Mr. Smith, would you mind repeating that direction now that Susan is listening so nicely?"*

Bottom line

To summarize, *Parrot Paras, like their namesake, engage in mindless repetition with no original thinking.* Not only is this type of support unilateral, but in the case of ASD, it also teaches to the individual's weakness, given these students' predilection for *visual,* as opposed to *auditory* information. *Bottom Line:* When one considers all of the accommodations and educational supports that could be used to facilitate the student's attention, participation, and successful performance, the Parrot Para just doesn't have the wherewithal to get the job done. Enter, the *Know-It-All Para*, in Figure 7.

I find these paras downright offensive, for the *fundamental*

Figure 7

The Know-It-All Para

problem here is not so much a matter of lack of knowledge—although that certainly can and often does loom large—as it is a matter of ego and attitude. Know-It-All Paras are true thorns in all persons' sides—teachers, therapists, parents, program consultants, and most of all, students, for they let you know, either directly or indirectly, that they are the keepers of all knowledge. As such, they act as though they have no need for input from classroom teachers, nor anyone else for that matter. Neither do these paras feel obliged to amass knowledge about their students' disabilities, for in their own exalted opinions of themselves, they *already* know it all!

 A thorn in everyone's side

These paras would be difficult enough to deal with if indeed they did possess an enviable knowledge base. This, however, is rarely the case. More often than not, the haughty attitude is a subterfuge for lack of knowledge, or caring, or both. Dealing with these paras can be extremely frustrating. For example, I once had a conversation with a Know-It-All Para in which she systematically rebuked each and every one of my recommendations. I had been called in to address a problem behavior vis-à-vis a young boy's resistance to participating in morning circle. I suggested several ways to entice the child's participation through the use of visual supports. To every one of my recommendations the para replied, *"I already do that."* Since none of the supports were in evidence on the day of my visit, I had to wonder why this para would wait until the school district hired an out-of-district consultant to stop doing what she "already" does!

Bottom line

These types of problem paras put enormous stress and strain on classroom teachers, since they behave as though they are above supervision and direction. *Bottom Line:* There is no place for this type of close-minded arrogance in the education of students with or without special needs. This para is best left outside the school house door, along with his or her inflated ego! Enter, the *Helicopter Para*, in Figure 8.

Like a helicopter hovering over a field site, these paras hover over their students at all times and in all activities. Unlike Know-It-All Paras whose sense of self-importance overshadows all else, Helicopter Paras are selfless in their mission to be all things to the students in their charge. But, just as *smother* love turns *mother* love into a hindrance, the hovering support provided by these paras *hinders*, rather than facilitates learn-

Figure 8

The Helicopter Para

ing, by creating *learned helplessness* and *prompt dependency* in students with special needs. This is especially problematic in the case of students with autism spectrum disorders, since they have a tendency to become dependent upon prompts even in situations where there is sensitivity to fading them back over time. Helicopter Paras are known for their physical proximity to their students, and for their highly intrusive prompts. I remember one such para "prompting" a preschool girl with autism through an exercise routine, moving her hands, feet, and eventually her whole tiny body in time to the music. The little girl dangled limply amidst the physical intrusion, with about as much involvement as a rag doll in the same situation. While intrusive physical prompts do little to facilitate the student's involvement in the learning situation, they do a great deal to promote *prompt dependency*. That is, the student comes to rely upon the para's physical prompt, rather than on his or her own ability to generate a response independently. When intrusive prompts occur over a long period of time they cause the students to tune out, turn inward, and quite literally "go through the motions," rather than become *involved* in the learning situation.

Not all intrusive prompts are physical, however. Sometimes Helicopter Paras use intrusive *verbal* prompts, as well. In this type of situation when the student is asked a question, s/he quickly learns to "hang in there" and wait for the (inevitable) prompt. Consider the following scenario:

Typical Peer: "Hi Billy."

Helicopter Para: "*Say* 'hi to Bobby.'"

Typical Peer: "How are you doing?"

Helicopter Para: "*Say* 'I'm doing fine.'"

Typical Peer: "Where are you going?"

Helicopter Para: "*Say* 'I'm going back to the classroom.'"

Typical Peer: "Good-bye, Billy."

Helicopter Para: "*Say* 'good-bye Bobby.' "

It's as if this para has an automatic "say gene" to fit all occasions. Needless to *say,* with his Helicopter Para quite literally putting words in his mouth, why should Billy bother to gen-

The "care and feeding" of learned helplessness

erate his own!? Voilà, *learned helplessness.*

Bottom Line: **Even though well-intentioned in many cases,** *overbearing and intrusive support does little to facilitate independence and efficacy in the student with special needs.* More-over, it conditions the student to "drop out" and wait for the prompt—be it physical or verbal—a situation hardly conducive to promoting competence in these students. Enter, the *Invisible Para,* in Figure 9.

Bottom line

Figure 9

The Invisible Para

Lacking the "substance" to get the job done

The diametric opposite of the ever-present Helicopter Para, is the nowhere-to-be-seen Invisible Para. These individuals are only too happy to do errands for the teacher and attend to matters *outside* the needs of their students—anything that will keep them out of harm's way, so to speak. They may be found in corridors, school offices, and teachers' lounges in school systems throughout the country. When in the classroom, they are often found among the typical peers. But one thing is for sure, they won't be found in the proximity of the students they've been hired to support.

 Bottom line

For whatever reason—lack of interest, fear of getting hurt in behaviorally charged situations, and/or laziness—these paras fail to make contact with their duties, responsibilities, or their students. *Bottom Line:* Invisible Paras lack the "substance" to get the job done! Enter, the *Fire Fighter Para*, in Figure 10.

The Invisible Para actually sets the stage for the Fire Fighter Para, for out-of-range of their students' distress signals, Invisible Paras fail to see the cues that signal impending problems. In this type of situation, one thing invariably leads to another in domino-like fashion. Before you know it, the student explodes (behaviorally, of course), creating the need for the Fire Fighter Para. Often armed with the accouterments of their trade—knowledge of various behavioral support "holds," and a penchant for picking up the telephone and calling in reinforcements with a frantic *"Code something or other"*—

 Reinforcements have arrived

these quick-response paras are primed to "put out the fire" as quickly as possible, with nary a thought regarding the *reinforcing* effect their behavior may have on the student. Unfortunately, some students actually enjoy the attention of the Fire Fighter Para mobilized for battle, particularly when things get a little boring in the classroom. One particularly amusing situation occurred several years ago in a school where I used to work. A young man with moderate autism actually interrupted his tantrum to pick up the telephone and call in his own "reinforcements" via his *Code M* "distress" call. The smile on his face as the Fire Fighter Para arrived to do battle appeared fleetingly, just before he resumed his

 Bottom line

tantrum! *Bottom Line*: Watch for signs of impending "disaster" and step in *before* the behavior escalates and the "troops" are mobilized. Enter, the *Traffic Cop Para*, in Figure 11.

Figure 10

The Fire Fighter Para

These paras direct the flow of all interactions in much the same way that traffic cops direct automobiles and pedestrians on a busy street. Their "fatal flaw" in the exercise of their duties and responsibilities is that they are *directive* rather than *facilitative*. For example, when a typical peer comes up to the child with special needs to ask to borrow a pencil, the customary reaction of the Traffic Cop Para is to answer for the child, rather than direct his or her attention to the typical peer and facilitate his/her response. Consider the difference between the following two scenarios.

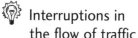 Interruptions in the flow of traffic

Situation 1:

Typical Peer: *"Cara, can I borrow your pencil?"*

Traffic Cop Para: *"Sure, Michael, here it is."*

Situation 2:

Typical Peer: *"Cara, can I borrow your pencil?"*

Para Pro: *"Cara, Michael asked you a question. Michael can you repeat your question now that Cara is listening?"*

Typical Peer: *"Can I borrow your pencil, Cara?"*

Cara: *"Okay."*

In the first situation, the Traffic Cop Para *directs* (i.e., takes full charge of) the entire encounter, actually responding for the student. Cara isn't even part of the interaction. In the second, the Para Pro *facilitates* Cara's attention and involvement so that she becomes an *integral* part of the interaction. The latter takes more time, but the results are well worth any time and effort that it may take.

Traffic Cop Paras are particularly troublesome for students with autism, as these students typically will not enter into, nor sustain interactions without caregiver support (i.e., facilitation). *Bottom line*: Because of their *directorial* job performance, Traffic Cop Paras miss rich opportunities, both in school and on the playground, to facilitate interactions between children with special needs and their classmates. Worse yet, by usurping the interactive role of the child, they

 Bottom line

Figure 11

The Traffic Cop Para

actually block interactions from occurring—a situation that is incongruous to the needs of all students with special needs, and particularly inimical to the interests of those with ASD. Enter, the *Automatic Pilot Para*, in Figure 12.

A "flight plan" out of sync with "ground" conditions

These paras perform their duties as though they have been programmed by some outside force over which they have no control. Their motto is to get the job done *at all costs*. Unfortunately, the costs are often too high for their students, both in terms of comfort level and degree of involvement. These are the paras that insist that the student have fun in 30 minute time blocks (whether they want to or not!) because it happens to be play time. They are *task-oriented*, rather than *student-oriented*. I once saw an Automatic Pilot Para use highly intrusive hand-over-hand support to "facilitate" a student's cutting, pasting, drawing, and totally completing the picture of a caterpillar, after which the para read a caterpillar poem, pasted it next to the "child's" picture, and told him that "he" had done a good job! During the entire time, not only were the child's eyes and face averted, there were also obvious signs of stress to which his para remained consummately oblivious. *Bottom Line:* Automatic Pilot Paras follow their own "flight plans" regardless of "ground" conditions—that is, irrespective of what's really happening in the trenches! This type of "support" runs roughshod over the child.

Bottom line

To summarize, the eight problem para prototypes discussed above, though based upon actual experiences that I have had with paras, have nonetheless been fictionalized and presented in humorous fashion so that they may serve as non-threatening prototypes whose foibles can be analyzed without offense to anyone. It is probably more common to find "combination" problem paras than the "purists" described above. What all problem paras have in common, however, is that they manifest distinctly human flaws that, if not *acknowledged* and *remediated*, can interfere with the paraprofessional's job performance, and hence with the educational care of the student. On the theory that it is often easier to learn from our mistakes than from our successes, it is hoped that the problem para parodies will serve a valuable instructional purpose.

Figure 12

The Automatic Pilot Para

Before discussing a model for caregiver support, there is one other para prototype to consider: Enter, the *Para Pro*, in Figure 13—that *para paragon par excellence!* (I'm sure you get the point).

The para paragon par excellence!

The true Para *Pro* meshes the art and science of paraprofessional support into a seamless, holistic tapestry in which the whole is infinitely greater than the sum of its individual parts. These paras have an almost intuitive understanding of their students' needs, having amassed a good deal of knowledge about both the students themselves and the disabilities they manifest. Unencumbered by the flaws besetting problem paras, Para Pros perform their duties and responsibilities flawlessly. They are true artists when it comes to analyzing situations and making judgments. Para Pros seem to have an endless supply of energy, as well as visual and other supports in their arsenals, and they know precisely when and how to use these supports to maximize student learning. Most importantly, they have mastered the art of reading their students' cues, so that, unlike the Automatic Pilot Para, they make the changes needed to accommodate their students' needs. In contrast to Helicopter Paras, Para Pros promote independence by only stepping in when additional supports and prompts are needed to facilitate their students' attention and participation, stepping back when less intrusive supports and prompts will suffice. Unlike Space Cadet Paras, these paras go about their duties and responsibilities *mindfully*, instead of *mindlessly*. Likewise, unlike Parrot and Traffic Cop Paras, they facilitate attention to, and participation in tasks, rather than merely repeat what the teacher just said, as in the case of the former, or direct interactions, as in the case of the latter. In contrast to Invisible and Fire Fighter Paras respectively, Para Pros are neither invisible when "the going gets tough," nor available only as reinforcements when "the tough get going!" Finally, Para Pros evidence a willingness to learn that the Know-It-All Para shuns as unnecessary. Para Pros also maintain excellent working relationships with classroom teachers and specialists alike, and are considered integral members of their students'

Bottom line

educational teams. *Bottom Line*: Para Pros achieve the difficult-to-achieve delicate balance required to fulfill their ultimate responsibility—that of providing *preeminent support in the educational care of their students*, a role which true Para Pros elevate to art form status.

Figure 13

The Para Pro

A Model for Caregiver Support

For aspiring para pros who need a bit more guidance with respect to decision-making, Figure 14, the *Transactional Interaction Model for Educational and Behavioral Support (TIM)*, provides a schematic representation to illustrate the levels of caregiver support involved in promoting and/or accommodating the student's growing independence in both the areas of skill development and behavioral functioning. Its underlying premise, like the term *transactional* implies, is that caregiver and student behavior is *interdependent;* that is, each person is influenced by, and in turn influences the other.

In this model, I have placed the student at the center of the universe, so to speak. The concentric circles surrounding the student illustrate both his/her stage of independence / behavioral appropriateness (represented by the letters), and the accompanying level of caregiver support required at each particular stage (represented by the numbers). The arrows serve to illustrate that *both the level of behavioral/skill development and the degree of corresponding caregiver support are bidirectional.* In other words, the level of independence exhibited by students for particular skills will vary, depending upon context and circumstance. Consequently, *different* levels of caregiver support will be required at *different* times. The same holds true for behavioral intervention. The following examples may help to clarify these points. In a "high stim," distracting environment, Mary would probably need more intensive educational support than she requires to perform the *same* task in a more hospitable environment (i.e., low stim, distraction free). The same holds true for behavior; that is, in an environment where stimulation and distractions are high, Mary would likely need more intensive *behavioral* support, as well. Similarly, *different skills also require different levels of caregiver support*, depending upon student variables (e.g., interest/motivation), and environmental circumstances (i.e., hospitable vs. inhospitable). Hence, Mary may require virtually no support to work at a *preferred* computer activity, but highly intensive support to sustain interactive play on the playground. So too, the degree of behavioral support would most likely reflect the varying demands of the different situations. *Bottom Line:* Caregiver support for *both* skill development and behavior is necessarily *fluid*, and should vary based

 Bottom line

Figure 14

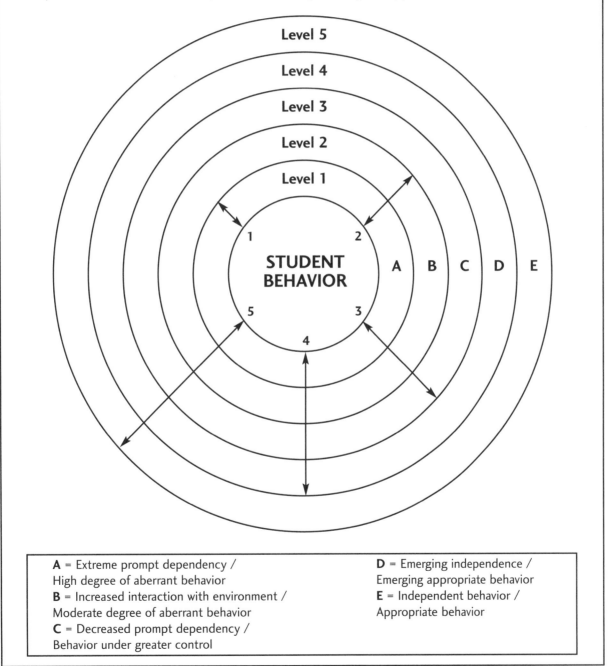

Transactional Interaction Model for Educational and Behavioral Support (TIM)

Schematic representation to illustrate the accommodation in caregiver support that is necessary as the student begins to behave more appropriately and exhibit greater independence. The alphabetical letters represent both the *student's* level of independence, and degree of behavioral appropriateness. The numbers refer to the concomitant level of *caregiver* support required at various stages. Note that as the student becomes more independent, and/or as behavior improves, the intensity of caregiver support diminishes.

A = Extreme prompt dependency / High degree of aberrant behavior
B = Increased interaction with environment / Moderate degree of aberrant behavior
C = Decreased prompt dependency / Behavior under greater control
D = Emerging independence / Emerging appropriate behavior
E = Independent behavior / Appropriate behavior

Adapted from the Sociocommunicative Interaction Model, Twachtman, 1990.
Copyright © 1999 by Starfish Specialty Press.

upon student needs and environmental conditions.

Decisions regarding the degree and type of support required are of necessity made by the person closest to the student. In many, but not all cases this will most likely be you. This is no small order, for during the course of a typical school day there are myriad instances which require caregiver support adjustments vis-à-vis student functioning. Thus, the level of support will vary considerably throughout the day, depending upon the particular task or activity, the degree of student competence, the quality of environmental conditions, and factors intrinsic to the students themselves (e.g., fatigue, discomfort related to sensory issues, etc.). Knowing when and how to modify support, though an *art form* in and of itself, is nonetheless informed by the *science* of understanding your particular student and his or her disability, as well as your ability to read the student's behavioral cues.

A Blueprint for Student-Driven Caregiver Support

The *Transactional Interaction Model for Educational and Behavioral Support (TIM)* is designed to serve as a blueprint for providing caregiver support that is *matched* to student needs. To determine your student's stage of skill development for a particular task or activity, you will need to consider four important issues: 1) the student's *level of familiarity* with the task / activity in question; 2) his/her *level of understanding*; 3) the student's *level of perceived relevance or interest*; and, 4) *internal factors* affecting student performance (e.g., sensory / health issues). If one or more of the first three factors is at a low level, and/or if internal factors loom large, chances are that a relatively *high* degree of support will be required to facilitate the student's attention and participation. If, on the other hand, one or more of the first three parameters is at a high level, *less* support will probably be needed to entice the student's attention and participation in the task or activity.

Determining stage of skill development and behavioral functioning

While the *TIM* is very easy to apply—and eminently logical in both its conception and use—it is important to keep a few points in mind. For one thing, the model is *student driven*; that is, it is designed to flow from student behavior and consequent need, to caregiver support, rather than the other way around. Stated differently, *paras are required first to determine the student's stage of skill development/behavioral functioning, and then to apply the level of support needed to sustain student performance and behavior.* Paras should neither mindlessly apply too much or too little support, as in the respective cases of the Helicopter and Invisible Paras, nor should they *arbitrarily* select a particular level of support, and then expect student behavior to follow. Another thing to keep in mind is that too much, or too long-standing Level One support can (and often does) create prompt dependency and learned helplessness. Similarly, a preponderance of Level Five support (which basically means not enough support, ala the Invisible Para) also works against student independence.

If you think logically you won't go wrong. Low skill development and/or aberrant behavior, combined with the student's comprehension difficulty or low interest, requires greater support than high skill development and/or appropriate behavior combined with good understanding and/or high interest. *Bottom Line*: In determining the level of educational support required to facilitate and maximize learning, *follow your student's lead, and adjust your interaction/teaching style accordingly.* Moreover, in order to mitigate against prompt dependency and learned helplessness—two behaviors out of sync with independence and competence—it is necessary for the Para Pro to *strive always to fade back prompts* when student attention, participation, and general performance can be sustained with less intrusive support.

Bottom line

Before moving on to the next chapter, it is important to note that the *TIM* can serve two very important functions when used in conjunction with a learning / behavior contract. On the one hand, it can be used in the *designing* of contracts, since the model enables caregivers to determine the level of support required vis-à-vis the degree of behavioral difficulty. This information is important with respect to specifying the terms of the contract. The *TIM* can also be incorporated into an "action plan" for fading back behavioral support as student behavior improves.

To summarize, the *TIM* provides paras and teachers with a blueprint for determining the amount of support to render for both skill development and behavioral regulation. When used in combination with adequate record keeping, it can also provide information regarding the student's progress toward achieving independence and competence. The importance of this cannot be overstated, since level of performance alone is *insufficient* to judge progress, especially if performance is *only* possible under conditions of intrusive support. Also needed, is a means for gauging the extent to which the student is becoming more *independent* in both skill development and behavioral functioning. The *TIM* provides caregivers with a tool for doing precisely that.

Take Home Message

- *Technical proficiency* without true *understanding* can take you only so far in rendering support to students with special needs.

- A blend of *both art and science* is needed in the educational care of students with special needs.

- Problem paras often *impede,* rather than *facilitate* student learning.

- Para *Pros* have mastered the *art and science* of paraprofessional support.

- The *Transactional Interaction Model for Educational and Behavioral Support* provides a blueprint for matching level of caregiver support to stage of student skill development and behavior.

Chapter Eleven

Sample Supports and Accommodations for Students with Special Needs

The vignettes which follow are intended to "breathe life" into the various types of supports and accommodations discussed in Chapter 9, and to set forth a blueprint for Para Pros to follow as they determine the support needs of their students. Most of the vignettes address common situations which confront paras who render one-on-one support to students with cognitive impairments. All of the examples address the needs of students with autism spectrum disorders, since these students typically manifest symptomatology and behaviors that are enigmatic and difficult to interpret. Even so, many of the supports and accommodations recommended are also appropriate for students with other disabilities, as well. Furthermore, the *Blueprint for Troubleshooting Problem Situations* is readily applicable to *all* students with special needs. A blank copy of this form may be found at the end of this chapter.

Peripheral Supports

Vignette 1

Problem Situation: Bobby is a 15-year-old student with ASD. He always seems to be a step or two behind his classmates. He is often late for class, and seems inevitably to be missing one thing or another—a writing implement, a necessary notebook, or his homework. When these things occur, Bobby becomes "frazzled," missing much of what goes on in the first ten or fifteen minutes of class. Sometimes, this is enough to "ruin" the whole day for him.

Troubleshooting: A diagnosis of ASD carries with it difficulties in executive function. Bobby manifests classic symptoms of EF deficits: disorganization, forgetfulness, and general unreadiness.

Action Plan: Since students with EF deficits benefit from visual supports to keep information "on line," the following supports and accommodations can be extremely helpful:

- A checklist regarding materials to bring to each class

- An assignment notebook

- Color-coded pocket files for each subject to aid Bobby in accessing specific assignments in a timely fashion

Role of the Para Pro: Consult the *Transactional Interaction Model for Educational and Behavioral Support* to determine the student's level of functioning and consequent requirement for caregiver support in the use of organizational aids. Chances are, *in the very beginning, the student will be quite dependent upon you to oversee use of the various supports* noted above. As the student becomes more acclimated to their use, you will need to *gradually* fade back your prompts over time.

Common Para Errors:

- Misinterpreting the student's behavior as resulting from laziness or noncompliance

- Expecting the student to become independent in the use of organizational supports immediately

- Relying upon verbal prompts and failing to provide the necessary organizational aids and supports

- Failing to fade back prompts over time

Vignette 2

Problem Situation: Molly is a 7-year-old student with moderate autism. Her long-standing difficulties with transitions have been helped considerably by use of a picture schedule which she consults at the beginning and end of each activity. She continues to have difficulty with *unexpected* change, however, particularly when the latter affects a *preferred* activity. Recently, Molly had a major tantrum when she was informed by her para that instead of going to see Ms. Smith, her occupational therapist (and one of her favorite people), she would be going to the auditorium for school pictures.

Troubleshooting: Individuals with autism prefer sameness, and hence have considerable difficulty with change, particularly when it is *unexpected*. This is especially problematic if the change involves moving from a *preferred* activity to either a *nonpreferred* activity, or one for which the student has little or no understanding or interest.

Action Plan: Since it is impossible to keep things the same all the time, *it is important to give students with ASD a way to anticipate and deal with change.* This can be done by putting a "change" symbol up over the picture of the affected activity. I use a cut-out of a lightning bolt for this purpose since, for students with ASD, change comes "out of the blue," not unlike the way lightning strikes.

Role of the Para Pro: In the beginning, helping students with ASD to understand the role of change in their lives will require pretty intensive support. Consequently, the Para Pro should set up several contrived situations involving change, *before* expecting the student to become comfortable with it. When doing so, it is important to stack the deck in the student's (and your!) favor. *Initially, structure change so that it moves from a nonpreferred activity to one that is more pleasurable for the student.* For example, if the student does not like recess, put the change symbol over the recess picture. Don't wait for recess time to mention the change in schedule. Rather, *go over the schedule the first thing in the morning— well in advance of recess.* When you come to the picture of the latter say, *"Oh look. There's a lightning bolt over the recess picture. That means there's going to be a change in the schedule. Today, instead of recess, we're going to go to the OT room and swing on the platform swing."* As you verbalize this, replace the recess picture with the picture of the swing. By going over the schedule in advance you *prepare* the student for the change so that s/he can *anticipate*, rather than be surprised by it. Further, by starting with change that involves pleasurable activities, the student comes to view change in a more positive light.

Common Para Errors:

- Viewing the student's resistance to change (e.g., tantrum) as a matter of noncompliance, rather than one of discomfort

- Waiting until the last minute to inform the student of the change, and then only using words to convey the message

- Failing to use visual supports

- Spending too little time helping the student to become comfortable with change

Vignette 3

Problem Situation: Michael is a 4-year-old boy with Asperger syndrome. His main difficulty is that he is constantly blurting out answers or shouting out questions during morning circle. His teacher finds this very annoying, as he constantly has to interrupt what he is saying to remind Michael to raise his hand. Even though Michael *immediately* raises his hand at the teacher's directive, soon after, he is back to blurting out answers! The teacher is frustrated because he feels that Michael is being non-compliant by not listening to him. For this reason, Michael spends much of circle time in time out, thus missing valuable instructional time.

Troubleshooting: A diagnosis of ASD carries with it difficulty in executive function. Impulsivity is one of the deficits in EF that is often seen in students with ASD (and ADD/ADHD, for that matter). By blurting out, Michael is demonstrating his *impulsivity*. By raising his hand immediately, in response to his teacher's directive, he is demonstrating his desire to *comply*. By *not* being able to sustain this behavior, however, he is demonstrating difficulty holding the directive in short term memory so that he can *apply* the correct response (i.e., raising his hand). These problems, too, are a result of deficits in executive function.

Action Plan: Cut out a circle that is red on one side and green on the other. Place a picture of someone with a finger to the lips (i.e., the universal gesture of silence) on the red side, and a picture of a boy raising his hand on the green side. These pictures can be photographs or line drawings. Put the two-sided circle on a piece of yarn so that you can wear it around your neck.

Role of the Para Pro: Practice wearing the circle with Michael, instructing him as follows: *"Michael, I know that you have trouble remembering to raise your hand, so I'm going to help you. See this circle—one side is red, and one side is green. When you see the red side—because red means STOP—you need to be quiet. To remind you of this I put a picture of some-one showing you that you need to be quiet. But , when I turn the picture over to the green side—because green means GO— it will be Michael's turn to speak. But look at the picture. See the little boy raising his hand? That's to remind you to raise your hand, Michael."* Your role does not end there. You also need to do the following:

- Stage practice sessions where Michael has to use the circle as a cue to control impulsivity

- "Train" the teacher in the technique, for he will have to remind Michael several times to look at the circle as a cue for behavior

- Cue Michael during circle time

- Fade back prompts

Common Para Errors:

- Thinking that the circle is somehow magic, and that mere-ly wearing it once or twice will "cure" the problem!

- Failing to "teach to the tool" by reminding the student to look at the pictures

- Starting out with the red side, and hence the more difficult behavior for the child to control

- Leaving the red side out too long, and the green side out too short a time

- Expecting independence too quickly

- Failing to fade back prompts

- Not reinforcing the child for his successes

Vignette 4

Problem Situation: Jenny is an 11-year-old girl with moderate autism. She has a penchant for always wanting to be first. When she has to be second or third in line, or when she can't be first in gym class or other activity, she becomes extremely upset and refuses to participate in the activity altogether. Her resistance is often quite disruptive to the other students.

Troubleshooting: When students with ASD are unable to understand the way things work, they often make up their own set of rules for dealing with inexplicable situations. Perhaps Jenny has an internal "rule" about always having to be first. Or, perhaps she doesn't understand that she will *still* get a turn and be able to participate even if she is not first. Whatever the reason, rest assured she has one—one that *makes sense to her*, even if it doesn't make sense to us.

Action Plan: You may never know the reason for Jenny's insistence upon being first. The important thing is to recognize that she does have a reason, and that it is *important* and *valid* to her. What is needed here is some way of *validating* her desire to be first, while letting her know that it's okay not to be first. It would also be helpful to provide her with a means for judging her place in line or in the order of turns.

Role of the Para Pro: An ideal first step would be a *Social Story*, both to recognize Jenny's desire to be first, and to provide her with important information that helps her to understand that it's okay to not always be first. An excellent second step—and one that helps to fortify the message conveyed in the *Social Story*—is to use what I call the old "Deli Counter" routine. In other words, explain to Jenny that her place (in line or in the order of turns) will be determined by the number she selects. Even though the *Social Story* will "set her up" to be more hospitable to this support, she nonetheless may resist at first, particularly if a number other than one comes up. If this is the case, follow the time-honored principle, *"If at first you don't succeed, try, try again!"* When you do, be sure to use the following language input, *"Jenny, you chose the number 3. The rule is you have to be number 3 in line today."* In my experience, there is something almost magical about the phrase, *the rule is*. Perhaps it is its definitiveness, or that it comes very close to the way individuals with ASD try to figure out the world. Whatever the case, use the phrase, *the rule is* wisely and well to give the student boundaries for what must seem to him or her an infinitely *boundless* world.

Common Para Errors:

- Viewing the student's desire to be first as stemming from selfishness

- Characterizing the student's resistance as mere noncompliance

- Failing to find a way to promote greater understanding and flexibility through the use of visual or other supports

Direct Instruction / Academic Support

Vignette 1

Problem Situation: Keith is a 7-year-old boy with Asperger syndrome. He is quite perfectionistic, often resisting participation in activities until he is sure he can "get it right." His exceptional strengths in math and computers, are being overshadowed by his fine motor problems and his perfectionism. He has a difficult time managing a pencil, and tries to avoid all activities which require this. One math assignment directed him to draw a circle around each correct answer. This was the scene of a major tantrum.

Troubleshooting: Students with Asperger syndrome often have fine motor problems, making use of a pencil difficult and labor-intensive. When combined with a tendency toward perfectionism, fine motor difficulty may also cause the student to resist activities which require it, since he cannot meet the impossible standard he has set for himself.

Action Plan: It's not up to you to specifically address Keith's fine motor problems, since his teacher and occupational therapist should be looking into it. Your mission is to *entice* the student's participation in the math assignment. What is needed here is an *accommodation* so that Keith can demonstrate what he knows *without discomfort.*

Role of the Para Pro: School supply rooms often have small metal rings for holding papers together. These rings can be used by Keith as ready made circles to surround the answers to the problems so that he doesn't have to draw his own.

Common Para Errors:

- Not recognizing the reason for the student's resistance as his lack of comfort with the task

- *Assuming* that the student's resistance to a task is merely a matter of noncompliance

- Failing to see the need for accommodations

- Viewing accommodations for the student's disability as "giving in"

- Setting up a power struggle!

Vignette 2

Problem Situation: Sam is a 14-year-old boy with Asperger syndrome. He is excellent at computational and rote math skills. Notwithstanding his strengths, he has significant difficulty with math *word* problems. His resistance to them has caused no end of grief, not only for him, but for his teacher, as well. Currently, his class is working on percentages. Although he receives extra help in the resource room, Sam has little interest in this subject.

Troubleshooting: Students with autism and Asperger syndrome often demonstrate excellent rote math skills, manifesting difficulty with abstract concepts and word problems. Further, these students generally resist subjects that they either find difficult or uninteresting, as is the case with Sam.

Action Plan: The "hooks" that work for typical students (e.g., "If you don't finish your math you won't be able to go out for recess), tend not to work for those with ASD. Hence, it is important to find ways to entice their interest.

Role of the Para Pro: Find out what Sam is interested in and build math tutoring activities around them. For example, if Sam is interested in the weather, design examples and/or build word problems around percentages related to the weather. Sometimes, this is a matter of using the examples in the student's math book, and substituting words to reflect student interest. Problems could also be constructed around the percentage of days that were sunny or rainy in a given time period, or those that were above or below a particular temperature. This is an activity that often requires teacher input. Consequently, be proactive in enlisting the teacher's help in creating the math problems, and be sure to use them in your pre- and post-teaching sessions.

Common Para Errors:

- Viewing the student's resistance to activities which he finds unmeaningful or uninteresting as simply a matter of noncompliance

- Not going the extra distance to build math examples around the student's interests

- Not keeping the teacher informed, nor enlisting his/her help

Vignette 3

Problem Situation: Sara is an 8-year-old girl with mild to moderate autism. Her reading *decoding* skills are excellent. In fact, they're well above grade level. Until recently, it was *assumed* that she also comprehended what she read. Unfortunately, this was not the case. Recent testing revealed that *comprehension* is an area of significant weakness for Sara, lagging well behind her excellent decoding ability.

Troubleshooting: It is not unusual for students with ASD to demonstrate *hyperlexia*; that is, advanced decoding skills (i.e., word recognition) with little or no comprehension. Moreover, *comprehension difficulty is an area of significant difficulty for individuals with autism spectrum disorders,* requiring specific, ongoing attention throughout the school years.

Action Plan: The *Story Line Organizational Support (SOS)* form located at the end of this chapter can be used to "pull out" and highlight important information that *Sara's disability precludes her from uncovering on her own.*

Role of the Para Pro: The *SOS* contains the following headings: *Title of Story; Author; Setting; Overview of Story; Character Descriptions; Story line Synopsis*; and *Synthesis*. In order to use the *SOS*, someone will need to read the books that Sara is required to read, and fill out the information requested. Given the child's "tender age," this should be relatively quick and easy. Share the *Story Line Organizational Support* form with the teacher so that s/he can determine who is best suited to generate this information. Even if this responsibility is not assigned to you, your role is nonetheless important, for you will need to *review* the information on the form with Sara to be sure that she understands it. In other words, you will use the tool to *directly teach* Sara the multifaceted task of comprehension, later "talking her through" the story and using the pictures to further fortify the establishment of meaning.

Common Para Errors:

* Being blinded by the student's decoding strengths, and *assuming* comprehension

- Relying on *testing* comprehension (i.e., asking questions), rather than *teaching* it (i.e., supplying information).

   Caution: Remember, if you keep asking the *same* question, and the student doesn't have the answer, it is not the student who is the slow learner! *Change* what you do. *Teach* (i.e., *supply the information*) rather than *test* (i.e. simply ask questions).

- Viewing a tool like the *SOS* as "giving the answers"

Vignette 4

Problem Situation: Mark is a 7-year-old very capable little boy with high functioning autism. Although he has significant strengths in math and computers, he has serious deficits in social skills. He is a loner both in the classroom and on the playground. Because of your excellent "advance work," you learn that in a few days Mark is going to have to write an essay on how to make a friend.

Troubleshooting: Establishing friendships is an area of significant difficulty for students with ASD. Thus, they would not have the requisite skills to bring to such an assignment, without specific attention and "advance work" on the caregiver's part.

Action Plan: This is a subject that, at the very least, will require a good deal of *pre-teaching*. It may even require some curricular modification in the way of assignment of a new topic. If this is the case, however, it is the teacher who will need to make that decision.

Role of the Para Pro: If pre-teaching is selected as an initial step, check out the library for some books on friendship and do some pre-teaching regarding friend-making behavior. Remember, *pre-teaching* means providing lots of information, not simply reading a book and asking questions. As noted earlier, the latter is *testing,* not teaching. If it is your job to write in the home-school communication book, enlist the parents' support by sending the book home and asking them to fortify the concepts presented in school. If writing in the book is not one of your responsibilities, ask the teacher if s/he will so inform the parents.

If in your pre-teaching activities it becomes apparent that the concept of friendship is too difficult for Mark to grasp, *discuss your concerns with the teacher* so that s/he can determine whether the assignment needs to be modified. While curricular modifications are within the purview of certified staff, *bringing such matters to their attention is a very important part of your job.*

Common Para Errors:

* Failing to do "advance work"

* Making curricular modifications without teacher input

* Failing to see the need for pre-teaching

* Failing to keep the teacher informed

Social, Play, and Leisure Supports

Vignette 1

Problem Situation: Lisa is a 9-year-old girl who is functioning in the moderate range of autism. She will play some simple board games with typical peers, but has trouble with turntaking. This is especially apparent when she has to lose a turn, or when someone gets two turns in a row—occurrences which often cause her a good deal of frustration. As such, Lisa is *dependent* upon her para's verbal prompts to take a turn.

Troubleshooting: Students with ASD have well-known difficulty with reciprocity; that is, in understanding the give and take required in taking turns. This is because the concept of turntaking is too abstract for them to grasp without support.

Action Plan: Anything that can be done to *concretize* the abstract concept of taking turns will help Lisa to participate in such activities more effectively.

Role of the Para Pro: Cut out a small circle and write the words, *My Turn,* on it. Explain to Lisa that when the circle is on her side, that means that it is her turn, and when it is on her classmate's side, it will be his or her turn. But, don't stop there. At first, you will need to prompt Lisa by *physically* assisting her in moving the circle back and forth between her partner and her. When it becomes obvious that Lisa has grasped the idea of using the turn marker with your physical support, it is important to *fade back to a less intrusive gestural prompt*, such as pointing to the marker. Use the *Transactional Interaction Model for Educational and Behavioral Support* as a guide for determining how and when to back off support. An additional advantage of the turn marker is that it can be used as a visual cue for verbal responding. For example, you can ask Lisa, *"Who's turn is it?"* while pointing to the words on the turn symbol, thus prompting her (unobtrusively) to say, *" My turn."*

Common Para Errors:

- Relying exclusively on verbal prompts for turntaking

- Expecting independence in use of the turn marker even before the student becomes accustomed to using it

- Failing to fade back prompts as the student becomes more independent

Vignette 2

Problem Situation: Alex is a 10-year-old boy with a diagnosis of Asperger syndrome. He has a lot of difficulty on the playground because he doesn't know how to approach other children. Often he will run up to a group of boys or girls as they are playing. The other children think that Alex is trying to spoil their fun.

Troubleshooting: Sometimes children with Asperger syndrome evidence socially excessive behavior without the perspective taking skills to determine the *effect* of their "exuberance" on other people. Even though Alex simply wants to play with his classmates, they view his behavior as off-putting.

Action Plan: This problem situation needs to be addressed from a couple of standpoints. In other words, both the class-mates' reaction to Alex, and his socially excessive behavior need to be considered.

Role of the Para Pro: You should inform the teacher of the classmates' reaction to Alex, as s/he may want to discuss their behavior with them. If you are skilled in writing *Social Stories*, or feel comfortable in using *Story Frames*, either technique may be used both to increase Alex's *social understanding*, and to guide him in more appropriate *social responding*. If you are uncomfortable in generating stories, ask the teacher or another staff member for help, for even if you don't generate these stories, it is important that you review them with your student. Once written, these stories are not only easy to review with students, but also very effective.

Common Para Errors:

- "Blaming" the child for his socially excessive behavior

- Inadvertently encouraging the typical peers to *patronize* the student by "playing on their sympathy"

- Failing to inform the teacher of the situation

- Failing to recognize the need for specific intervention

- Viewing the *Social Story* or *Story Frame* from a "one or two shot" perspective, as opposed to supports which require *sustained* efforts over time

Vignette 3

Problem Situation: Alison is a 4-year-old child with mild to moderate autism. She wanders about the preschool classroom during free play flapping her hands, reciting nursery rhymes, and singing songs like *Mary Had a Little Lamb*. Attempts to re-direct her to the doll or other play area have been futile.

Troubleshooting: First and foremost, remember the adage, *There is no such thing as free play for children with autism!* When left to their own devices, children with ASD will often engage in self-stimulatory and repetitive behavior.

Action Plan: Fortunately, Alison's interest in nursery rhymes and children's songs is not only age-appropriate, it can form the basis for interactive social and play skills development.

Role of the Para Pro: Your "front and center" role with Alison gives you the perfect opportunity to follow her lead, in terms of her interests, and build interactive skills around her. There are several options here. By using her interest in nursery rhymes and songs as a catalyst, it may be possible to facilitate some interactions between her and other children in an activity she truly enjoys. To begin with, find a typical peer or two, and together with Alison lead them in a rousing rendition of *Mary Had a Little Lamb*. Since *all* children love repetition, repeat this activity several times. Try introducing other interactive songs over time, such as *London Bridge, Old MacDonald Had a Farm, Here We Go Round the Mulberry Bush*, and similar action songs. In addition, since Alison likes rhythmic activities, try some chants and rhymes such as *One, Two, Buckle My Shoe*. As she becomes more comfortable with the proximity of her classmates, assist her in acting out some nursery rhymes during the time devoted to free play. For example, if you were using the rhyme, *Little Miss Muffet* you would need someone to role play Miss Muffet and the following props: a pillow (for a tuffet), a bowl (for curds and whey), a rubber spider, and your spirited theatrical direction! The children can take turns playing Miss Muffett.

Common Para Errors:
- Leaving the child to her own devices
- Failing to follow the child's lead in terms of her interests
- Leaving the development of play skills to chance

To summarize, the sample supports and accommodations discussed above are only a few of many such techniques in the educational care of students with autism and other disabilities. Hopefully, they will serve as a springboard for your own creative ideas. The important thing to remember is to follow the blueprint for determining the specific supports and accommodations which your students need:

- Identify the problem situation

- Engage in troubleshooting

- Develop an action plan

- Assume an active role, and modify plan as needed

- Be aware of common para errors

Bottom line

Bottom Line: Even when certain educational decisions are not yours to make, the *expertise* that you've developed in reading your students' signals and identifying their needs can go a long way toward supplying teachers with the information they need for informed decision-making.

Take Home Message

- Approach problem situations with an *open mind*, and *reserve (behavioral) judgments*!

- Analyze problem situations, taking into account *knowledge of both the student and his or her disability.*

- *Develop an action plan* based upon the student's needs.

- Be *proactive* in the application of supports.

- Keep the teacher *informed* and *involved.*

Blueprint for Troubleshooting Problem Situations

Use the "how to" vignettes presented in Chapter 11 as a guide to completing this form. The information contained within this manual will be helpful in the troubleshooting phase.

Student: _____ Respondent: _____ Date: _____

I. Define the Problem Situation
(Include *specific* information regarding student behavior, context, and other relevant variables.)

II. Troubleshooting Guide
(Use your *knowledge* of the student and his/her disability to list factors that may be contributing to the problem. Be sure to consider the following areas: communication and language; social understanding and expression; interests; sensory issues; perspective-taking ability / empathy; executive function / organizational ability; degree of environmental support. Using a "best guess" strategy, develop a hypothesis regarding the possible cause(s) of the problem.)

III. Action Plan
(List the steps to take to address the problem. Be *specific* regarding all accommodations, modifications, and supports.)

IV. Follow-Up
(Modify Action Plan, as needed, to accommodate student and situation.)

Story Line Organizational Support
(S.O.S.)

I. **Title of Story**

II. **Author**

III. **Place Where Story Occurs**

IV. **Overview of Story**

V. **Character Descriptions**

A. **Main Characters**

B. **Supporting Characters**

VI. **Story Line Synopsis / Supporting Commentary**
(Can be page-by-page for young children, or chapter-by-chapter for older students)

VII. **Synthesis**
(Highlight imbedded information; e.g., inferences; abstractions; idioms; social-emotional information, including the attribution of mental states; etc.)

Chapter Twelve

A Wrap Up Potpourri
Melding Art with Science

"A child is not a computer that either 'knows' or 'does not know.' A child is a bumpy, blippy, excitable, fatigable, distractible, active, friendly, mulish, semicooperative bundle of biology. *Some factors help a moving child pull together coherent address to a problem; others hinder that pulling together and make a child 'not know.'*" [emphasis supplied]

S. H. White

This quotation is as applicable to teenagers as it is to children. Moreover, it may have even greater relevance for students with special needs than it has for those who are considered typical. The Take Home Message for trench people is that *there are things that we, as caregivers, can do to help students understand and learn, and there are things that we can do to hinder learning and prevent students from understanding and knowing.* Consider the following interaction in which an eighth grade girl with mild autism (and obvious literalness) is being questioned about a paragraph that she has just read aloud:

Caregiver: *"So, where are we?"*

Student: *"In the room."*

Caregiver: *"No. Where are we in the story"*

Student: *"At the beginning."*

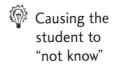 Causing the student to "not know"

Caregiver: *"No. Where are we in the story?"*

Student: (Silence; signs of anxiety)

Caregiver: (Exasperatedly) *"What's the setting?"*

Student: *"The circus."*

If this caregiver had known that students with autism are *literal*, she would have either asked the question differently to begin with, or she would have realized the "error of her ways" after her student gave the first answer. As a witness to this interaction, I am certain that this caregiver never did understand her student's literalness, since—as noted in the quote at the beginning of this chapter—*what she did (i.e., the way she phrased her question), caused her student to "not know."*

 Bottom line

There is another lesson to be learned from this interaction—one that should be obvious, but somehow isn't in actual practice: *It is only when the caregiver phrases the question in a manner that enables (facilitates) student understanding that the student is able to be successful. Bottom Line:* We *inadvertently* teach students to *not know* when we fail to make the adjustments necessary in *our* behavior to *accommodate their understanding* and *enable learning.* Perhaps another somewhat different, but related example will suffice to underscore how easy it is to *disable* learning.

An 11-year-old boy with Asperger syndrome was feeling ill at school one day; hence, the following interaction:

Student: *"I feel like I'm going to throw up."*

Para: *"Let me go tell the teacher."*

Teacher: *"Do you feel like you're going to vomit?"*

Student: *"What does that mean?"*

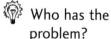 Who has the problem?

Teacher: *"It means you feel like you're going to throw up."*

Student: *"But that's what I said."*

Teacher: *"Well, let's go to the nurse's office."*

Nurse: *"Do you feel nauseous?"*

Student: *"What does that mean?"*

Nurse: *"It means you feel like you're going to throw up."*

Student: (At this point, quite frustrated) *"But that's what I said!"*

So, I ask you, who has the problem—the student with the disability that *precludes* his having a flexible understanding of how *different* words can mean the *same* thing (particularly when in the throes of illness!), or the adult caregivers who fail to see how *their* questioning helped him to *not know*?! Given the time lost in meaningless interrogation, the only positive aspect of this entire interaction is that the student managed to not throw up!

In my workshops I compare the rendering of educational care to students with special needs, to that of operating a sailboat. Those who sail have no control over the weather, nor the direction or speed of the wind. They do, however, have control of both the helm by which to steer the boat, and the sails by which to propel it through the water. Likewise, in working with students with ASD and other special needs, there are many things over which you as paras or other caregivers have little or no control. But, like the hypothetical sailor, you too are at the "helm" of your students' educational "ships", for it is your job to provide them with the supports they need to find their way to greater competence and independence. Finally, like the sailor who manages the sails, the decisions you make, and the care with which you execute your responsibilities, can either propel your students forward, or stagnate their educational progress. May the care you render enable your students to "stay the course" toward educational success!

"Staying the course" toward educational success

My purpose in writing this manual has been a dual one: first, to drive home the point that *what we don't know about students and their disabilities can and will impede their learning;* and second, to provide you with both *basic information* to aid your understanding, and *practical strategies* to translate that understanding into appropriate and effective action. The rest is up to you. Hopefully you have read, and will heed the Take Home Messages interspersed throughout this manual, for they constitute the essential points for each of the major topics covered. Given their importance, they are categorized according to subject matter, and reprinted as a unit in Appendix A. May they add to your knowledge base by providing you with the critical information you need in a ready-to-access format, so that you may perform the important job you've undertaken with the care and sensitivity it deserves. So too may you consider the following "commandments" your "mission statement":

THE TEN COMMANDMENTS OF PARAPROFESSIONAL SUPPORT

 The Para Pro's mission statement

1. Thou shalt know well both your students and the disabilities that they manifest.

2. Thou shalt learn to take your students' perspectives, and realize that they have significant difficulty taking yours.

3. Thou shalt always look beyond your students' behaviors to determine the functions that those behaviors serve.

4. Thou shalt be neither blinded by your students' strengths, nor hold them to standards they cannot meet.

5. Thou shalt master the art of rendering the appropriate degree of support for your students' level of skill development and behavior.

6. Thou shalt exercise vigilance in fading back prompts and promoting competence and independence in your students.

7. Thou shalt be proactive both in seeking out information to help your students, and in preparing and implementing the supports that they need to be successful.

8. Thou shalt neither usurp the teachers' role, nor be albatrosses around their necks.

9. Thou shalt leave your egos at the school house door!

10. Thou shalt perform your duties *mindfully, responsibly,* and *respectfully* at all times.

It is my profound hope that you will take to heart your "mission statement," for *what* you do, and *how* you go about doing it, are of paramount importance in the educational care of the students you serve. May the information contained within this manual, together with the examples, forms, and instructional ideas, provide you with the support *you* need, so that you may render the support your *students* need to achieve success in school. Finally, may you perform your duties and responsibilities in a manner that *enables* your students to *know*. As a true Para *Pro,* how could you do otherwise?!

The true
bottom line

Take Home Message

- There are things that paras and other caregivers can do to *help* students understand and learn, and there are things that they can do to *hinder* learning and *prevent* students from understanding and knowing.

- We inadvertently teach students to *not know* when we fail to make the adjustments necessary in *our* behavior to *accommodate their understanding* and *enable learning*.

- The care that you render can *enable* your students to "stay the course" toward educational success!

Appendix A

COMPENDIUM OF TAKE HOME MESSAGES

PART ONE: AUTISM SPECTRUM DISORDERS "101"

Getting Down to Basics

- The first most basic building block of appropriate educational programming is *knowledge of both the disability and the student who manifests it.*

- *Ignorance is not bliss!*

- In-service education for paraprofessionals should be *comprehensive* and *continuous.*

- From a "big picture" perspective, *what is best for neurotypical children is not only best for children with autism, but also for all children with special needs.*

- *Individuals with autism are operating with their best efforts at adaptation* under difficult conditions, given their neurological challenges.

- In order to effectively meet the needs of students with autism, it is necessary to *view the world from their individual perspectives.*

- *With power goes responsibility*—first to *learn,* then to *apply* information in a manner that *facilitates,* rather than impedes learning.

Getting Acquainted with the Autism Spectrum Disorders Continuum

- *Autism exists on a continuum* from mild to moderate to severe.

- *Autism is a spectrum disorder* which incorporates varied but similar conditions.

- The term *autism spectrum disorder (ASD) encompasses the entire continuum.*

- Autism can and does exist *with* and *without* mental retardation.

- *Make careful observations,* not assumptions, particularly when judging ability level.

- Autism spectrum disorders are *neurological,* not psychological or environmental.

Perspectives on Social Behavior

- There is *always* a problem in social behavior in autism spectrum disorders.

- *Atypicalities in social behavior are bidirectional,* and may take the form of *"deficits"* (i.e., lack of social interest and/or socially motivated behavior), or *excesses* (i.e., one-sided, nonreciprocating, approach behavior).

- Problems in social behavior affect the student's ability to *understand* a social situation, and hence to generate a skilled (i.e., appropriate) social *response* to it.

- *Social understanding* is the basis for appropriate *social expression.*

- Students with Asperger syndrome are more likely to manifest symptomatology marked by *social excess.*

- *Students with ASD are not rude!*

Perspectives on Communication and Language Behavior

- *There is always a problem in the use of language for social communication purposes (i.e., pragmatics),* regardless of the student's level of functioning or type of pervasive developmental disorder.

- *It is common to be blinded by the strengths of more able students,* and hence attribute to them a higher level of communicative competence than exists.

- *Communication always develops before language,* even in individuals with ASD.

- Insisting on longer and longer utterances *before* the student is developmentally ready to produce them may produce anxiety and frustration.

- *Comprehension precedes meaningful expression,* but it should never be merely *assumed.*

- *Students with ASD have difficulty with all three areas of pragmatics:* the *functions* of communication (e.g., requesting, protesting, etc.); making *social judgments* by which to regulate the flow of information; and understanding and abiding by *conversational rules.*

- Two of the most common caregiver errors in ASD are *assuming communicative competence,* and *mistaking problems in communication for problems in behavior.*

- *All* behavior communicates!

A Look at Interests and Imagination

• Students with ASD demonstrate a *narrow range of interests* that are often *unusual* in nature, and a *restricted repertoire of activities* that reflect their *preference for sameness.*

• These characteristics are not conscious choices, but rather *symptoms* of their disorder.

• Since students with ASD have as little control over their interests as neurotypical students do, *it is up to paras and other caregivers to find "hooks" to entice their interest and participation.*

• When play behavior is present in ASD it tends to be *impoverished.*

• *Atypicalities in imagination, like those in social behavior, are also bidirectional;* that is, imagination may be characterized by *too much,* as can be the case in Asperger syndrome, or *too little,* as in the case of less able children.

• There is no such thing as *free play* for students with ASD!

Toward Understanding Response to Sensation

• Abnormal *sensory input* equals abnormal *motor output.*

• Sensory impairment in ASD can be characterized by *oversensitivity* (e.g., tactile and auditory defensiveness); *undersensitivity* (e.g., absence of pain); or *short circuits"* (e.g., synesthesia).

• There is *significant variability* with respect to the *number and type* of sensory anomalies, and the *manner* in which they are manifested both among and within students with ASD.

• *Fatigue* and *anxiety* (on the negative side), and *comfort level, motivation,* and *trust* (on the positive side) contribute to the *"on again, off again"* quality of sensory impairment in ASD.

• To avoid erroneously classifying sensory issues as behaviorally-based, *always look beyond the external behavior that you see,* in order to determine whether or not there is an *internal,* sensory-based component to it that you cannot see.

Demystifying Theory of Mind and Perspective Taking

• Perspective taking is a *shared* phenomenon: Our ability to take the student's perspective is *crucial* to his/her success.

• Students with ASD have significant difficulty with *perspective taking, empathy,* and *theory of mind.*

- Theory of mind deficits in ASD interfere with the student's ability to *size up* a situation.

- Students with ASD have *significant difficulty dealing with the ambiguities involved in making inferences and predictions, and in dealing with nuances,* all of which are required in ToM activities.

- *Theory of mind tasks require social understanding and social judgment*—areas of *profound difficulty* in students with ASD.

The Role of Information Processing

- Current research shows that *students with ASD have significant difficulty with information processing.*

- Information processing glitches may occur *anywhere* in the system.

- Abnormalities in one part of the system negatively impact functioning in another, given the *interdependence* among processes.

- *Slow* and/or *deficient processing* in students with ASD leads to *problems in information retrieval and use.*

- Information processing is dependent upon the *integrity of the executive function system* which oversees it.

Perspectives on Executive Function Mechanisms

- Executive function deficits in ASD can cause the following discrete symptoms: *distractibility; impulsivity; inflexibility / rigidity and transition difficulty.*

- Discrete deficits, in turn, create problems in higher-order activities such as *problem solving and mental planning; organizational skills, self-monitoring, and application of skills.*

- *Interest in a task or activity helps to maintain attention* and stave off distractions.

- Don't assume that because a behavior is exhibited in a relatively simple and *supported* environment, that the student is capable of *executing* or *self-monitoring* that same behavior in a more complex and less protected "real world" environment.

- Likewise, don't assume that the student *understands* the need for the behavior in the natural situation.

- *The student's significant and pervasive problems in planning and organization should never be mistaken for laziness or noncompliance.*

- Students with ASD require *special understanding* and *special supports* that address their planning and organizational needs.

High Functioning Autism or Asperger Syndrome?

- Autism and Asperger syndrome are considered *different expressions of the same basic disorder.*

- While high functioning autism and Asperger syndrome *share many similarities,* there are also *important differences* in the presentation of symptoms.

- Students with Asperger syndrome "inhabit" a topsy turvy world, given that the willful and volitional *appearance* of their behavior leads to *misunderstanding* of their motivations.

- Despite *qualitative* differences in the presentation of symptoms, students with high functioning autism and Asperger syndrome share *similar educational needs.*

PART TWO: THE "ART AND SCIENCE" OF BEING A PARA *PRO*

Perspectives on the Basics of Paraprofessional Support

• Your first responsibility is to *understand both the student and the disability s/he manifests.*

• It is vitally important that you obtain information about the student's learning style, needs, and preferences.

• The maintenance of confidentiality in *all* matters is a top priority.

• *Be proactive* with respect to seeking out information regarding what is expected (and what is not!).

• Do what is necessary to *establish and maintain a relationship of trust with the teacher.*

• Strive for *balance* in your role of *preeminent support.*

• *Check your ego at the school house door!*

The Role of Peripheral Supports

• *Peripheral supports provide crucial supplements* that have the power to *enable* student learning.

• *Visual, organizational, and time management supports are required* to shore up executive function ability in students with ASD, ADD/ADHD, as well as those with other learning disabilities that adversely affect executive function ability.

• *Students with ASD need highly directive support* if they are to learn the things that their disability *precludes* them from learning without support.

• Paras assisting in the implementation of therapy plans should *exercise extreme care in carrying them out according to the therapist's specifications.*

• If it is not forthcoming, *paras should be proactive in seeking continual direction from therapists in the implementation of therapy programs.*

The Role of Direct Instruction and Academic Supports

• There is a great deal of *overlap* between peripheral and direct instruction / academic supports.

• Effective decision-making regarding the selection and use of appropriate supports requires *constant vigilance* and a *keen understanding* of the student's specific needs.

- Pre- and post-teaching are mainstays of paraprofessional support, and *absolute requirements* in the case of ASD.

- Familiarity breeds *attempt!*

- Modifications / adjustments in task presentation can help to *facilitate* successful performance.

- Adjustments with respect to curricular requirements are within the purview of *certified* staff.

- On-the-spot modifications and adjustments have their place, but *they should not supplant preparation and planning.*

- Breaks should be used *judiciously,* and paras should assume the responsibility for bringing students up to date regarding what they missed.

The Role of Social, Play, and Leisure Supports

- *Paras play an important role in the generalization and maintenance of social, play, and leisure skills.*

- "Free Play" should be a time when paras *set up and facilitate important social and play behaviors.*

- *Social Stories* and *Story Frames* can help to *increase social understanding as a means of promoting appropriate social expression.*

- *Story Frames* may also be used as a *direct academic* support for interactive story telling.

The Role of Behavioral Supports

- Always ask yourself the question, *"Which came first, the behavior or some frustrating or aversive situation that may have caused it?"*

- *Problem behaviors* are not the same as *behavior problems.*

- Behavioral supports may serve an *indirect* or *direct function.*

- The wise use of *indirect* supports can *minimize,* and in some cases *eliminate* the need for more direct supports.

- By exercising *vigilance,* it is possible to prevent *problem behaviors* from becoming *behavior problems.*

- Academic, social, play, and leisure supports may help to *prevent* behavioral disruption.

- Learning / behavior contracts provide students with ASD with a *"road map"* for understanding and negotiating the complex social world.

- Exercise extreme care so as not to *inadvertently* reinforce inappropriate behavior.

- *Behavior management provides a short-term strategy* to handle a problem, whereas *behavior modification promotes long-term change.*

- Situations involving behavioral difficulty require *team input.*

The Importance of Clerical and Record Keeping Responsibilities

- Record keeping activities are an *integral* part of the student's programming, providing important information regarding *progress, setbacks,* and a *road map for future planning.*

- There is a place for both *qualitative* and *quantitative* data.

- Be *proactive* in seeking out the information you need regarding *IEP goals* and *objectives,* and the *content* of lessons and activities.

- Haphazard, sloppy record keeping *compromises* student learning.

- *Share information* with the classroom, special education, and special area teachers at regular intervals.

- *Special* education *requires* the use of *specialized* educational supports!

- Paras need to assume a *proactive* role in the use of educational supports for students with special needs.

Blending the Art and Science of Paraprofessional Support

- *Technical proficiency* without true *understanding* can take you only so far in rendering support to students with special needs.

- A blend of *both art and science* is needed in the educational care of students with special needs.

- Problem paras often *impede,* rather than *facilitate* student learning.

- Para *Pros* have mastered the *art and science* of paraprofessional support.

- The *Transactional Interaction Model for Educational and Behavioral Support* provides a blueprint for matching level of caregiver support to stage of student skill development and behavior.

Troubleshooting Problem Situations

- Approach problem situations with an *open mind,* and *reserve (behavioral) judgments!*

- Analyze problem situations, taking into account *knowledge of both the student and his or her disability.*

- *Develop an action plan* based upon the student's needs.

- Be *proactive* in the application of supports.

- Keep the teacher *informed* and *involved.*

The Para's Role in *Enabling* Learning

- There are things that paras and other caregivers can do to *help* students understand and learn, and there are things that they can do to *hinder* learning and *prevent* students from understanding and knowing.

- We *inadvertently* teach students to *not know* when we fail to make the adjustments necessary in *our* behavior to *accommodate their understanding* and *enable learning.*

- The care that you render can enable your students to "stay the course" toward educational success!

ULTIMATE TAKE HOME MESSAGE

Read and *heed* the Take Home Messages for they will help you
to enable learning!

Appendix B

ANNOTATED RESOURCE LIST

The following materials contain a great deal of practical, and in some cases *directly applicable* information for working with students with ASD and those with other special needs. They represent a compilation of both reference materials and direct programming ideas. Please share this list with teachers, clinicians, and parents.

Organizational Support Material

Learning to Learn: Strengthening Study Skills and Brain Power by Gloria Frender; ISBN # 0-86530-141-7.

- Contains a wealth of information regarding organizational, reading, test-taking, and thinking skills

How To Reach and Teach ADD/ADHD Children by Sandra F. Rief; ISBN # 0-87628-413-6.

- Contains practical strategies and techniques for working with individuals who have attention / executive function problems

Peripheral / Behavioral Support

Visual Strategies for Improving Communication: Volume 1: Practical Supports for School and Home by Linda A. Hodgdon, M.Ed., CCC-SLP; ISBN # 0-9616786-1-5. Available from QuirkRoberts Publishing, P.O. Box 71, Troy, MI 48099-0071.

- This manual contains a panoply of visual supports and examples to aid *all* who work with students with special needs. It is appropriate for parents, as well.

Solving Behavior Problems in Autism: Improving Communication with Visual Strategies by Linda A. Hodgon, M.Ed., CCC-SLP; ISBN # 0-9616786-2-3. Available from QuirkRoberts Publishing, P.O. Box 71, Troy, MI 48099-0071.

- This manual is an excellent reference for approaching problem behaviors from the perspective of communication. It contains a wealth of practical strategies and visual supports.

Direct Academic Support

Making Social Studies Come Alive: 65 Classroom-Tested Activities and Projects by Marilyn Kretzer, Marlene Slobin, and Madella Williams; ISBN # 0-590-96381-3.

- Covers grades 4 - 8. It contains some excellent ideas and presents them in ways that are motivating to students.

Math Magic For Your Kids by Scott Flansburg; ISBN # 0-06-097731-0.

- This book is intended for elementary school students. Some of the material is more directed toward the younger student; however, I recommend using this as a supplement to the regular math curriculum, as it presents math concepts in visual and motivating ways.

Mind Joggers: 5- to 15-Minute Activities that Make Kids Think by Susan S. Petreshene; ISBN # 0-87628-583-3.

- Covers math, language, writing, and reasoning activities. An excellent resource for students in grades K – 6.

Social, Play, and Leisure Support

Social Stories by Carol Gray. Available from Future Horizons, Inc. (1-800-489-0727).

Comic Strip Conversations by Carol Gray. Available from Future Horizons, Inc. (1-800-489-0727).

- The previous two resources are excellent for addressing the social and social-emotional issues that loom large for students with ASD and other special needs. When used according to instructions they provide invaluable social-emotional support for students.

Homemade Books to Help Kids Cope by Robert G. Ziegler. Available from APA (1-800-374-2721).

- A superb, user-friendly resource for addressing social and social-emotional issues in a visual format. This one is especially good for younger children, and those who are nonreaders. This tool can also be used for *direct academic support* as noted in *How to be a Para Pro*.

Guess Who? A Game by Milton Bradley

- An excellent resource for working on attributes, and for socialization, since it can be played with a peer.

Play & Imagination in Children with Autism by Pamela J. Wolfberg; ISBN # 0-8077-3814-X.

- A wonderful reference that goes a step beyond the important role of play in the development of children, by examining the critically important domains of play and imagination in those with autism.

Toys To Grow With: Infants & Toddlers by John J. Fisher; ISBN # 0-399-51243-8; Perigee Books; The Putnam Publishing Group.

- An excellent resource for play ideas to make learning fun. Contains 50 age-graded toys that parents and educators can make in minutes.

Neurotypical Peer Education

Captain Tommy by Abby Ward Messner. Available from Future Horizons, Inc. (1-800-489-0727).

- A charming story about a little boy with autism and his neurotypical peer buddy. Appropriate for grades 1-4.

Trevor Trevor by Diane Twachtman-Cullen. Available from Starfish Specialty Press. Internet: www.starfishpress.com. Toll Free: 1-877 STARFISH (877-782-7347).

- A metaphor designed to be read to children by adults. *Trevor Trevor* is designed to increase the sensitivity of typical peers toward their classmates with disabilities without labeling the disability. Special features include the use of two Trevor paper dolls for story line review with children. Since the disability is not identified, the story can be used for children whose parents are uncomfortable with labels. Appropriate for grades 2 - 5.

Miscellaneous Support and Reference Material

Autism Society of America. 7910 Woodmont Avenue, Suite 300, Bethesda, MD 20814. Toll Free: 1-800-3 AUTISM or (301) 657-0881. Fax-on-demand: 1-800 FAX-0899.

- *The* clearing house for a large variety of information on autism spectrum disorders, and sponsor of the ASA National Conference.

The Morning News, edited by Carol Gray. Subscriptions are available from Jenison High School, 2140 Bauer Road, Jenison, MI 49428. Telephone: 616-457-8955.

- A superb international publication that gets to the very heart of ASD. Contains invaluable information for *everyone* in the trenches.

The MAAP. Available from Maap Services, Inc. P.O. Box 524, Crown Point, IN 46308.

- An excellent quarterly newsletter for families of more advanced individuals with ASD.

Books That Build Character by William Kilpatrick and Gregory and Suzanne M. Wolfe; ISBN # 0-671-88423-9.

- An excellent annotated bibliography of books that teach moral values through stories. This book is for reference only.

Relaxation: A Comprehensive Manual for Adults, Children, and Children with Special Needs by Joseph R. Cautela and June Groden; ISBN # 0-87822-186-7.

- The exercises in this manual are easy to do and designed to decrease anxiety.

The Perigee Visual Dictionary of Signing by Rod R. Butterworth; ISBN # 0-399-50863-5.

- An excellent reference for the use of manual signs. The pictures are easy to follow.

The Time Timer developed by Jan Rogers. Available from Generaction, Inc. (Toll Free: 1-877-771 TIME).

- An innovative and excellent way of depicting the passage of time *visually*. I feel that this is a *must* for every home and classroom, particularly for younger and/or less able children.

Index